CODING
BEGINNERS

LEARN COMPUTER PROGRAMMING
THE RIGHT WAY

By K. Connors

© Copyright 2017 By K. Connors - All Rights Reserved.

Copyright © 2017 *Coding for Beginners.* All rights reserved. No part of this publication may be reproduced, distributed, or transmitted in any form or by any means, including photocopying, recording, or other electronic or mechanical methods, without the prior written permission of the publisher, except in the case of brief quotations embodied in critical reviews and certain other noncommercial uses permitted by copyright law. This also includes conveying via e-mail without permission in writing from the publisher. All information within this book is of relevant content and written solely for motivation and direction. No financial guarantees. All information is considered valid and factual to the writer's knowledge. The author is not associated or affiliated with any company or brand mentioned in the book, therefore does not purposefully advertise nor receives payment for doing so.

Table of Contents

PART ONE 7

COMPUTER PROGRAMMING FOR BEGINNERS 7

INTRODUCTION 8

CHAPTER ONE 13

WHAT IS COMPUTER PROGRAMMING? 13

CHAPTER TWO 21

WHAT CAN YOU DO WITH COMPUTER PROGRAMMING? 21

CHAPTER THREE 25

UNDERSTAND THE BASICS OF COMPUTER PROGRAMMING 25

CHAPTER FOUR 30

COMPUTER PROGRAMMING CONCEPTS FOR BEGINNERS 30

CHAPTER FIVE 39

COMPUTER PROGRAMMING AND PROGRAMMING LANGUAGES 39

CHAPTER SIX 49

COMPUTER PROGRAMMING LANGUAGES CONTINUED 49

CHAPTER SEVEN 60

THE MATH INVOLVED WITH PROGRAMMING 60

CHAPTER EIGHT 68

ELEMENTS OF A PROGRAM SPECIFICATION 68

CHAPTER NINE 73

GAME PROGRAMMING 73

CHAPTER TEN 77

PROPERTIES OF A GOOD COMPUTER PROGRAM 77

CONCLUSION 84

PART TWO 88

LEARN PYTHON 88

INTRODUCTION 89

CHAPTER ONE 90

ALL ABOUT COMPUTER PROGRAMMING 90

CHAPTER TWO 105

WHAT IS PYTHON? 105

CHAPTER THREE 116

INSTALLING PYTHON 116

CHAPTER FOUR 119

PYTHON VARIABLES 119

CHAPTER FIVE 126

OBJECT-ORIENTED PROGRAMMING 126

CHAPTER SIX 148

WHY PYTHON? 148

CHAPTER SEVEN 155

HOW TO PROGRAM IN PYTHON 155

CHAPTER EIGHT 158

TIPS FOR LEARNING TO CODE THE EASY WAY 158

CONCLUSION 163

PART THREE 166

PROCRASTINATION 166

INTRODUCTION 167

CHAPTER ONE 172

WHAT IS PROCRASTINATION? 172

CHAPTER TWO 185

WHY DO WE PROCRASTINATE? 185

CHAPTER THREE 194

WAYS TO STOP PROCRASTINATING NOW 194

CHAPTER FOUR 203

IS IT LAZINESS? 203

CHAPTER FIVE 210

HOW TO END PROCRASTINATION 210

CHAPTER SIX 218

FIVE EMPOWERING PROCRASTINATION TIPS 218

CHAPTER SEVEN 223

MANY NEGATIVE EFFECTS OF PROCRASTINATION 223

CHAPTER EIGHT 233

PROCRASTINATION AS A CAREER KILLER 233

CONCLUSION 238

PART ONE

COMPUTER PROGRAMMING FOR BEGINNERS

INTRODUCTION

Before you jump in and start learning a programming language, it will be helpful to you if you understand what programming is and how it works, including some programming terminology. A computer on its own is just a useless box. It's nothing but a bunch of different hardware items assembled into a single unit. At this point, these hardware items either together or individually are of no use. This is as good as a car that has been assembled. Is the car of any use without fuel? In the same way, we need to provide the computer with fuel, in this case, its electricity. A computer at this point is essentially just a big bunch of tiny electronic switches that are either on or off. Now, this is as good as a car with enough fuel and can be driven, but no driver to drive.

We need a driver who can operate the steering wheel, gears, breaks, etc., which will make the car move around. In the same way by setting different combinations of these switches, you can make the computer do whatever you want. For example, play a video on the screen, or play music through the computer speakers, or open a file, etc. Now, telling a computer when to switch on these switches and when to switch off them is, in other words, nothing but instructing a computer what to do. This is what programming is, in very simple terms.

Programming often refers to computer programming. So, this now brings us to our first and most important question.

WHY LEARN COMPUTER PROGRAMMING?

Computer programming isn't just about building the next cool app, or about creating a killer website - it's about planning, discipline, and problem solving, as well as a good introduction to the wonderful world of logic. Even for people who are never destined to actually make a career out of telling a computer what to do, there are some great advantages to be had by acquiring the skills needed to actually do it.

Before looking at the three key skills that are common to all forms of programming; planning, problem solving and logic - it's worth recounting a little anecdote about the misconception that programmers have to be engineers, or at the very least, good at mathematics.

There was a time when computers were the size of a house and communicated with the programmers using little bits of cards and ticker tape. If they went wrong, someone had to repair the valves (yes, valves), and it saved a lot of time if that person was also the programmer.

LEARN PLANNING THROUGH COMPUTER PROGRAMMING

It is said that the best way to appreciate subject matter is to teach it to someone else. This being the case, the best way to appreciate how to do something well is to break it down into successively smaller steps until the whole process is laid bare. With knowledge of all the components, estimates of time and cost can then be applied, as well as the various checks and balances that will prove that what has been done has been done correctly, and is the correct thing to have done in the first place.

COMPUTER PROGRAMMING AS AN INTRODUCTION

TO PROBLEM SOLVING

Some things just don't seem possible at first glance. No doubt the idea that every page on the internet could be indexed, and then searched in real time was considered to be a bit of a pipe dream by some. However, knowing that a computer is just a thing that can interpret commands leads the programmer to be able to find a way to solve just about any problem. If there aren't any obvious solutions, the brain has a way of being able to think laterally and at least find a workaround. The basis of this is known as logic.

BASIC LOGIC IN COMPUTER PROGRAMMING

This is really the only "sciency" bit of programming left. Logic essentially allows you to hand the decision-making process over to the computer, and force it to perform different actions depending on the various conditions it encounters.

There are also logic constructs that let the programmer repeat actions, as well as choose actions, and ways that various lists of instructions can be reused for different tasks, depending on how they are invoked. Seeing the entire domain as a set of interacting objects in this way is a fundamental transferable skill that computer programming teaches.

In fact, all of these skills are transferable. Computer programming is one big set of transferable skills, and that's probably the best reason there is to learn computer programming.

CHAPTER ONE

WHAT IS COMPUTER PROGRAMMING?

Computer programming, commonly known as programming or coding, is the art of making a computer do what you want it to do. Programming in very simple terms is about writing programs. A sequence of instructions written to perform a specified task for a computer is known commonly as a program, but is also referred to as a software program or even computer program. A computer is just hardware that requires instructions to act upon. These instructions are executed by the computer CPU.

Programming is planning how to solve a problem. No matter what method is used - pencil and paper, slide rule, adding a machine, or a computer - problem solving requires planning.

Based on the above definition, programming is planning how to solve a problem. So, here we are not actually solving the problem, but the computer will do it for us. If we solve the problem ourselves, then there is no necessity to write a program, and hence, we don't require a computer to solve it.

Then why do we need a computer if we know how to solve a problem ourselves? Because we simply cannot do it at the speed and accuracy with which a computer can. Also, we may get tired and bored of doing the same job again and again, but the computer can do the same job a million times at the same speed and accuracy as the first one without getting bored or tired.

We can take a simple example of calculating the sum of all even numbers from 1 to 1,000,000. This is not something that we cannot do, but the time that is required to calculate, the possibility of making a mistake at some point of time, a number of resources required if we use a pen and a paper or a calculating machine, and other similar reasons make this an undesirable option. Over and above this, what if we need to calculate between a different set of numbers again and again? It is difficult humanly. However, by writing a program, we can achieve this in less than 5 minutes. At the same time, we can keep running the same program again and again for doing any number of calculations and get accurate results in seconds.

We can instruct the computer to take each number, add it to the next and from there on add every next number to the previous sum until we reach the upper limit specified. Don't look at these instructions for its accuracy, but what you need to understand here is that we can instruct a computer to solve a problem only if we know how to do it. This means that unless we know the solution to the problem, it's of no use even to try solving one.

You can take an example of a cab driver on the street, but who is new to the city. With this cab driver, we cannot simply get into the car and ask him to drive to point A. We will have to give him proper instructions on the route that he needs to take to reach the destination. We can give him the instructions on the route only if we know how. Otherwise, it will be a futile effort.

In the same way, there is no point even trying to write a program until you have the knowledge of how you are going to set about solving the problem. Put in simple words, programming is telling a computer what to do. Though it seems to be pretty simple, it's very complicated.

The very important point here is that computers don't speak English. Since a computer, being a machine, only understands two basic concepts: on and off. The on and off concept is called binary system with on representing 1 and off representing 0. Hence, the computer knows only one language that is of 0's and 1's, commonly known as binary language. The second important thing is that your instructions should be PRECISE. As we have mentioned previously, a computer on its own is just a useless box. It's nothing but a bunch of different hardware items assembled into one unit. So, if you have to instruct a computer, then you have to tell it PRECISELY what to do.

COMPUTER PROGRAMMING

Now we are going to present computer programming and discover how it may be applied to command the way your computer operates. Generally, computer beginners aren't concerned about controlling the computer, but are are commonly concerned in learning more about how it all works.

Nevertheless, they may be surprised to learn that computer programming increases computer knowledge as a whole and it can assist to decrease the fearfulness and intimidation associated with using a new computer.

Computer programming is creating a succession of commands that enable the computer to do some actions. The people who program computers (called computer programmers) use a programming language to communicate with a computer. You might have heard of some of these languages in the past such as Visual Basic, C++, Python, or Fortran. There are hundreds of other programming languages and neither one is better than the other. Just about all of them are capable of executing the same tasks and accomplishing the same goals. A programmer chooses one language by a simple preference.

Each of these languages differs by the way they communicate with a computer, and the commands that they abide by are very specific. Not a single command of one language can be exchanged with the commands or language of another. But all of them can be used to control a computer.

At present, it would be impossible to teach you how to program any language in a single book. However, we can still introduce you to some of programming's most basic concepts - starting with the commands. Commands are the instructions that a computer conforms to perform an action. To make them work inside of a program, programmers assign commands to objects like buttons, for example.

The commands in a program are pretty worthless unless they have some data to pursue, so programmers either give the programs some information to work with (a list of names or numbers for example) or they make the program generate its own data. Occasionally, the data comes from an outside source like the internet or the computer that the program resides. The data that a program receives is called input, and data that the program generates is called output.

Other times, the data is unknown. If the program were working with a simple algebra equation like, "$x + 5 = y$," the variables "x" and "y" would be unidentified pieces of data. Or if a program were to calculate a date "x" days from now, the variable "x"

would be an unidentified piece of data until we tell the program what "x" is. In programming, it's sometimes required to work with unidentified pieces of data.

That's when conditions are convenient; conditions allow a program to execute an action based on the event of a previous command. Using this type of command, we can instruct a program to do one thing if the "x" variable in our latter example turned out to be 9 days, and then do a different thing if the variable turned out to be 31 days.

Commands, data, variables, and conditions help build the most simple programs, and there are certainly more components of any programming language. But when they're typed into a programming language and compiled to create an executable file (a file ending with the .exe extension), they turn into a software application.

As we mentioned earlier, you can use a programming language to control your computer. By using simple commands, you can program your computer to perform mathematical tasks, fill out web forms, compose an email message and send it off, or any number of other things. If you're interested, you may find Visual Basic one of the easiest computer programming languages to learn. Visual Basic is an object-oriented programming language and it automatically codes much of a program the minute a programmer drags a button onto a screen.

CHAPTER TWO

WHAT CAN YOU DO WITH COMPUTER PROGRAMMING?

In summary; computer programming is the process of designing and writing computer programs. That sounds pretty straightforward, doesn't it?

At its most basic level, you can think of programming as giving instructions to a computer to do something you want it to do - which might sound very similar to how you operate your desktop computer. Simplistically, the only difference between what you are doing now as a computer user and what you might do as a computer programmer is that the instructions are saved somewhere so they can be used over and over. As a matter of fact, if you have used macros in a software program, like a word processor or spreadsheet (or countless other applications that are macro enabled), you have already done computer programming of a sort.

Programs can be as simple as a set of instructions

stored in a text file for doing some mundane task, like making backups of all the computer files in a folder, or as complex as something like a word processor, or the operating system that your computer uses which can require millions of lines of code. We need to understand that computers are generally just pieces of metal, plastic, silicon, and other materials stuck together in a way that allows them to do some amazing things that seem like thinking, can't actually think at all. But what they can do extremely well is follow instructions. So what are these instructions, anyway? At the level that a computer understands, these have to be very precise, very detailed, and very complete step-by-step directions, and they must be in a form that the processor and other parts of the computer can understand - and that is as little electrical pulses which humans aren't capable of emitting (at least not at this time).

In a way, you can think of a computer program like a recipe: a set of instructions that can be followed to produce a result. In the case of a recipe, the instructions are used by a human and can, therefore, be a bit descriptive, leaving out some of the details. For example, if a recipe instruction is to "pour the mixture into a blender and whip until frothy", it is assuming that the human knows what a blender is, and where it is, and how to set it up, and how to use it - and also what pour means, and what frothy means, and so on. The human chef is expected to fill in the gaps.

A computer can't do this - it has no idea what anything means, except for a few very simple instructions. The way we do this is to write instructions that can then be translated into something the computer can understand. The "way to write instructions" is called a programming language.

What a programming language allows us to do is to write instructions for the computer in a more or less human readable form, that can then be translated into something the computer can work with. The human readable instructions are typically called a code. Each line of human readable code translates into thousands of detailed computer instructions. A special program (or set of programs) is used to do this translation - each computer language has its own translators, which are called compilers or interpreters. Once the translation is done, the result is stored in some form such as a file or set of files (or in computer memory in some cases), and each time the software is run, the computer will follow the instructions and (hopefully) the program will do whatever it is that it is supposed to be doing.

Although it is often imagined that you have to be a genius to be able to write useful software, almost anyone who is computer savvy and has an interest in becoming a power user can learn to program. Most software is written by average people with specialized knowledge and skills. Mastering computer programming can be a lifelong pursuit, but gathering enough knowledge and skill to be able to write useful code isn't out of reach for anyone who knows how to use a computer and is willing to dedicate a little time... or maybe a lot of time, but still - it isn't out of reach.

CHAPTER THREE

UNDERSTAND THE BASICS OF COMPUTER PROGRAMMING

If you have used a computer for any purpose up until now, you may not agree with me, since you have been using it mostly in English or any other language that you know. You may have watched movies, listened to songs, created documents, sent emails, browsed a lot of sites, and you may even have read my articles, books etc. in one of these human readable languages. Also, if you have written a program or even seen somebody doing it, you might have noticed that even they have not been using the language of 0's and 1's.

Even if you agree that there are people who know this language of 0's and 1's, looking at the second important point, we said that "the instructions should be PRECISE", you might be thinking that it will be next to impossible to even write a simple computer program, if what I'm saying is true.

Today, to use a computer you need not know how a computer works or what language it speaks. All you need to do is simply turn on a computer and when it is ready to use the mouse and keyboard, point at some little graphical object on the screen, click a button (or swipe a finger or two in the case of a touch screen device) to get a computer to do what is required of it. An example would be what you need to read this book (if you're reading on a computer).

The reason computers are so easy to use today are because of the hard work of some programmers who have programmed for it to behave in a certain way. And here we are not trying to use a computer but to learn how to program a computer. But the computer doesn't know anything except for binary language; and remember not all computers speak the same dialect. That is the reason a program on a desktop computer does not run on an iMac and vice versa.

Let me explain with an example of two blind people, wherein the first person (let us call him as Person-A) knows only English and the other person (let us call him as Person-B) knows only French and is blind. Person-A wants Person-B to draw a sketch. Now, how do you expect these two to communicate with each other. Isn't it difficult? Person-A can't even show in writing since Person-B is blind.

The only way of communicating is through speech in a known language, and by giving precise instructions.

Now, the only way they both can communicate with each other is by having an interpreter. Now when Person-A speaks in English, the interpreter then translates it into French and repeats it to Person-B. When Person-B says something in French, the interpreter again translates and repeats the sentence in English to Person-A. Now, with the help of an interpreter, both are able to communicate very easily.

Using the interpreter solves our language problem. We still have another problem at hand: that is Person-A is asking Person-B, who is blind, to draw a sketch. Though this is not something that is impossible, it is difficult, unless you know how to instruct. Even if Person-A is able to now communicate, he should know the steps in a proper order and very precisely, otherwise he will get Person-B to draw something, but not what he would be expecting. Person-A should know every minute detail very precisely since Person-B is blind. He will just follow whatever Person-A instructs. If Person-A asks him to draw a line of 1.23 cm, from a particular point with a certain degree, Person-B without questioning anything, just does that without even thinking about the outcome. If Person-A knows how to instruct precisely and exactly in the way it is required, then Person-B will draw what he wants in the way he wants.

If we get back to computer programs and use the same approach as in the above example, everything becomes very simple and easy. Replace Person-A with yourself and Person-B with the computer. Now the first thing you need is an interpreter, and the second is knowing what you want and the precise steps that is required, so that you can get the work done.

To read or write a binary code or program is unfortunately very difficult for humans. So we have to use some kind of program that can translate something we instruct in English into Binary language and vice versa. These programs which can translate our instructions in English into Binary code are surprisingly called... wait for it.. an interpreter.

Do these interpreters really understand English?

This might be the question you're asking yourself, or not. Either way, the answer is yes and no.

Yes, since we use English words in programming languages, and no since computers are still not up to that level so as to understand what we speak, be it in any language. This type of language is known as high-level language. By using the term languages, we are not referring to various languages such as English, French, etc., but we're referring to the high-level languages that we use to write programs, which are then interpreted and converted into binary code so as to make the computers understand it.

CHAPTER FOUR

COMPUTER PROGRAMMING CONCEPTS FOR BEGINNERS

GETTING STARTED THE EASY WAY

A computer program is made up of a chain of instructions a computer has to perform. These instructions may come with other important data that's needed to carry out those instructions. Hence, the process of programming involves the defining of the instructions and the data. For you to come up with data for your computer, you should be familiar with computer programming basics and the three fundamental elements:

1.   Instructions that need to be carried out.

2.   Order in which the instructions are to be carried out.

3.   Data needed to complete the instructions.

The first stage of computer programming basically

involves paper processes. In this phase, you don't even need to work using a computer, however, if you use a word processor that will enable you to write your work to a disk file rather than on a piece of paper. You need to do this so you can figure out clearly and more specifically what you want your computer to perform before you begin to instruct the computer to execute it.

Bear in mind that the computer will follow the instructions exactly as given. It can't say what you want; it can rather do what you want it to do. So before your program comes close to a computer, you need to do several steps which include:

1.   DEFINING THE PROBLEM

Before you instruct the computer what to do, you must first be familiar with it. You need to clearly tell the computer what it needs to accomplish, or to generate as the outcome of all the activities it will perform.

2.   IDENTIFYING THE SOLUTION

If you already know what the computer will produce as an end result, you should take a close look at the information you have, and determine the information that you require. There's also a need for you to define the logical procedures, equations, and other methods you have to utilize so you can manipulate the raw input data into the end result you want to achieve.

3.   MAPPING THE SOLUTION

This stage in computer programming has to be laid out in proper order. Don't forget that the sequence in which actions are used is as vital as the actions themselves. When organizing the solution into the right order, you will be putting choices into consideration.

When you're done defining the problem as well as designing and mapping the solution, the next thing you need to do is the task of writing the program code into one or a couple of computer language(s). But before you proceed, you must first decide on the possible languages you need to use as well as the particular computer platform.

Usually, computer languages are optimized for various kinds of tasks. It is, hence, important to select first the language that will best suit the task required.

INSTRUCTING OR TELLING A COMPUTER WHAT TO DO

The process of instructing or telling a computer what to do is called computer programming. It involves writing valuable, sustainable, extensible commands that can be read by a computing system to do a significant task. Programming can be achieved using one or some of the different languages dubbed as programming languages as explained above.

Since one instruction is not enough for a computer to perform something substantial, you need to come up with a set of instructions, known as programs, and submit it to the computer to be able to complete a task. For beginners, learning programming concepts as well as the processes in making computer programs isn't a piece of cake; it requires know-how and programming skills.

The lowest form of coding a novice programmer can do is the machine code. This code is written in binary and it uses a series of "0's" and "1's".

However, just because it is known as the lowest form of code doesn't mean it is the easiest to do. Higher code forms like Java, C, and C++ are made to make it easier for anyone to learn and use compared to the machine code.

For beginners to know what they should expect, here are the procedures involved in computer programming:

1.   DEVELOPING A PROGRAM

In this stage, the programmer, whether novice or experienced, usually works with internet marketers, sociologists, or other individuals to find out the program needed by the market to be able to work better at home or in the workplace. The features of the programs are then created from the suggestions of the other people involved. It is the programmer who'll determine the feasibility of the suggested features.

2.   CHOOSING THE RIGHT LANGUAGE

Depending on the programs you need to develop and your knowledge of the language, you now need to select the right language you will use. Hyper Text

Markup Language (HTML) and Hypertext Preprocessor (PHP) are the two Internet languages commonly used by programmers. HTML is ideal if you are developing a basic web page while PHP is for the applications or things that you actually don't see happening. Other languages you can use are CSS, Visual Basic, MySQL, C, C++, Java, and many others. Programmers frequently use different languages in a single program since each of them has unique functions.

3. WRITING THE SCRIPT OR CODING THE PROGRAM

Once the features of a certain program are made final, the programmer should now start working on it. This involves coding the program or writing the script to perform particular actions by means of a computer language.

4. TESTING THE PROGRAM

After coding the program, it needs to be tested before it will be released. Programmers usually apply for this program in various operating systems to test its ability to function. If the program works well, it will then be released in beta version.

5.   TROUBLESHOOTING ERRORS

Along with the release of the program's beta version, is a request for users to report any bugs or errors they encounter so they can be fixed right away.

Computer programming is by no mean easy. You need to be armed first with the basics before you can move on to the next and more crucial steps. The best way to learn the ins and outs of computer programming and programming concepts for beginners is to read books, take classes, or listen to programming tutorials.

THINGS TO CONSIDER WHEN WRITING A COMPUTER PROGRAM

1.   SET UP THE LOGIC OF THE PROGRAM

Logic is considered the backbone of any program. It needs to be prepared based on the resources your chosen programming language allows. Preparing the logic must be done prior to the real coding process. You should make a flow chart for your program, or write its algorithm before you start with the process of writing the program.

2.   SPLIT THE PROGRAMS INTO FUNCTIONS

The majority of the programs let you break the program into functions. These functions need to be written with the least number of instructions. They must be designed in such a way that they can be reused over and over again.

3.   STUDY THE SYNTAX OF EVERY COMMAND YOU'LL USE

One of the reasons for most programming errors is an improper use of syntax. There are many programs that have features that can be used to check the syntax of each command as well as integral functions that you want to utilize.

4.   MAKE SURE YOUR CODE IS SHORT

The fewer the number of instructions, the faster the rate of execution of the program. Most of the time, we use complex logic in getting this task done.

Little do we know that this task can easily be performed if we utilize the built-in functions of the programming language. To avoid these problems, you should have enough knowledge of all the inbuilt functions available in the program.

5. BE SURE THAT VARIABLE NAMES AND FUNCTIONS ARE LOGICAL

Proper names used in functions and variables make the coding process simpler. While using illogical variable names won't impede the program's functionality, it will make it harder for you to enhance or modify this code afterward.

Aside from learning various programming languages, computer programming for beginners involves familiarization of the above-mentioned tips.

CHAPTER FIVE

COMPUTER PROGRAMMING AND PROGRAMMING LANGUAGES

In order to pass on instructions to computers, programming languages are used. These languages, which are designed by people, are based on the so-called rules of syntax and semantics. These days, a wide range of languages have been made, employed, and discarded.

Programming languages usually don't last that long. They come up but after just a few years of stay in the industry, you will feel that the language needs some improvement or you need something your chosen language can't provide. It won't be long until that particular language is replaced by a more flexible successor.

Programming languages do evolve because there's a continuous search for efficient transformation of human language into machine code. Languages produced usually start with ideas, which conceal hardware and employ representations that are more convenient to human programmers. Another crucial facet of language design is dealing with the program's complexity. As programs become bigger and more refined, developers have come to realize that there are language types that are easier to support in huge systems. Because of this, event-driven and object-oriented languages have become widely used.

TYPES OF PROGRAMMING LANGUAGES

Since this field is evolving, there is no set standard in categorizing programming languages. One way to characterize them is through programming paradigm. These classifications include:

1.   OBJECT-ORIENTED

Object-oriented programming isn't just the newest; it is also the most powerful among the paradigms. In programs that are object-oriented, the designer indicates the data structures as well as the categories of operations that can be done on it. The combination of data and operations that can be carried out is dubbed as an object.

2.   PROCEDURAL

Procedural programming involves a list of actions a program needs to accomplish to be able to attain a certain goal. This is a simple paradigm wherein a program is divided into a starting phase, list of operations that need to be done, and an ending stage. Also called imperative programming, procedural programming involves the idea of the procedure call.

3.   STRUCTURED

A unique type of procedural programming, structured programming offers additional tools that can be used to deal with the issues produced by larger programs. In structured programming, the program is split into small codes that can easily be understood. Oftentimes, structured programming is associated with a top-down approach which starts with an overview of the system.

Computer programming languages are artificial and are made to manage computers. To come up with a new and better language, the developer needs to spend hard work and long hours. With this introduction to computer programming, you've become familiar with the various types of languages based on paradigms.

INTEGRAL PARTS OF PROGRAMMING LANGUAGES

Are you new in the field of computer programming? If so, it is very important to know and understand the common concepts and principles involved in such a field. While computer programming for beginners comes with a certain level of difficulty, it is still achievable, especially if you are equipped with the basic principles and concepts.

Writing a program involves storing data as well as manipulating it by means of a series of instructions. Included in the data are time and countable factors such as names, dates, and descriptions. By means of data types, you'll be able to find out how data must be stored and used.

Most programming languages such as C, C#, C++, Visual Basic, and Java have integral parts which novice programmers need to get acquainted with.

Among such parts are:

1.   VARIABLES

Programmers have to understand that variables provide them with momentary storeroom for any information needed while the program is used. Variables also play a great role in moving information from one section of the program to another. There's also the so-called local variable which can be accessed or modified by a specified portion of a program and global variables which are accessible to any part of the program.

2.   DATA TYPES

Any computer language comes with data types because they help maintain the information contained in the program. However, programming languages have some restrictions on the data types they provide. Among the popular data types are characters, pointers, numbers, and strings. Numbers come in either floating points or integers. String data conceals internals that can be manipulated via exposed functions. Additionally, character data types stocks up numbers, symbols, letters, and spaces while the pointer is a piece of memory which can also be utilized for storing arrays.

3.   OUTPUT

Since it is an important part of any programming language, it is advisable that you have a good understanding of the various types of outputs in the majority of the computer programming languages. One of the popular types is text output, which provides a simple means of revealing the result of a particular computer program. Graphical output is a bit difficult and it needs higher resolution.

4.   TESTING CONDITIONS

These allow you to find out the path through a program by implementing a code with value as the basis. This value, which can be variable, another expression, or constant, is compared against an expression.

One example of a testing condition statement is "IF". In case the validations became unsuccessful, many computer languages let you define a chunk of code that needs to be executed using the "else" statement.

Aside from the indispensable elements of programming languages, computer programming for beginners also requires you to be familiar with the different language categories which include compiled languages, markup languages, and programming languages. It is also wise to have a full understanding of the general principles and concepts behind each and every programming language. All of these factors are very useful in helping you become an expert in a particular programming language or in computer programming in general.

BASIC LANGUAGES YOU CAN USE IN CREATING PROGRAMS

Individuals who want to learn computer programming and the languages that can be used in making programs must first be familiar with the basics. Languages employed in programming should be one of your primary considerations. Prior to creating programs, it is crucial that you know the different types and levels of programming languages. Among these are:

1.   MACHINE LEVEL LANGUAGE

We all know that computers work in bits and bytes and it reads and understands binary digits 0 and 1. While you are free to create a program in any language you like, it has to be transformed into the languages of 0s and 1s before it can be implemented.

It means you need to write a program or convert your written program into machine language. And this is no easy task. It is nearly impossible to memorize a long sequence of 0s and 1s for each instruction you wish to be executed. Yes, it is true that before the development of high-level languages, the ones used in making programming codes were machine level languages. These days, however, this level of language is not used anymore in designing computer programs.

2.   ASSEMBLY LEVEL LANGUAGE

This level of programming is only one level higher than a low level or machine language. This is actually the reason why creating a program using such languages isn't a piece of cake, although, the programming code produced is still understandable.

There are lots of programs for embedded technology that are created in assembly language. The program that's responsible for transforming assembly level programs into machine level programs is called the assembler.

3. HIGH-LEVEL LANGUAGE

These computer languages are easier for humans to understand. It entails clear statements for making each instruction. Languages that fall in this category have different purposes. There are languages designed for web programming, some for desktop applications, while others can perform both tasks.

One thing to bear in mind though: a high-level language isn't easy for the computer to understand. This is where the importance of an interpreter or a compiler comes into play. Such programs transform the programming code into a language form the machine can understand.

Aside from these three basic levels of languages, another generation of programming language is now being designed. This is dubbed as the fourth generation language which is designed for those who have very minimal or no programming experience.

Developers of such language want these inexperienced programmers to learn to prepare their own code. This is also the very reason why high-level languages like Java already came with these systems. These enable a person to write a programming code without memorizing every function.

Bear in mind that no matter what programming language you want to learn, you need to have a proper understanding of the basics. If you're not familiar with programming language basics, you will not be able to make a program in that specific language. It is advisable that you take up computer courses so you'll be able to learn more than just the basics of computer programming.

CHAPTER SIX

COMPUTER PROGRAMMING LANGUAGES CONTINUED

Programming computer languages typically belong to any of the two types - compiled and interpreted. Compiled programming languages are implemented by using compilers, which are translators that generate machine code from source code. The compiler can translate the source code into the intermediate form, which is known as byte code. In interpreted programming languages, the programs are not directly executed by the host CPU, but they are executed by a software program called an interpreter.

It is advisable to start with programming for beginners like BASIC. There are several basic compilers and interpreters, along with commercial programming like Visual Basics from Microsoft.

Though there are several types of BASIC, it is advisable to start with QBASIC. In order to run

QBASIC, you need to get to DOS and then find out the icon "MS-DOS". Double click on it so that you can get "C: //WINDOWS>. Type QBASIC and press the enter key. If you get a blue screen with something like a guide, it means that you are ready to program.

If you want to learn programming with a simple syntax, you can go for LOGO. LOGO is used for functional programming. It is known for its turtle graphics, which is a method of programming vector graphics by using a cursor. You can build more complex shapes like squares, circles, triangles and other figures with the help of this language.

Though there are many good beginner programming languages, it is worth selecting C, C++, BASIC and Java, which are great for learning and support. C is a popular programming language that has facilities for structured programming. It features a static type system to prevent unintended operations. C++ is a compiled general purpose programming language and is an enhancement of the C programming language. It offers more than 30 operators, which cover basic arithmetic, comparisons, logical operations, and manipulation. JAVA derives much of its syntax from C and C++.

The Java applications are compiled to byte code and they can be run on any JAVA virtual machine, irrespective of the computer architecture. Modula 2 is a great teaching language that is ideal if you want the power of C++ and the friendly syntax of BASIC.

It is advisable to have an Integrated Development Environment (IDE) that supports several languages for the purpose of editing, in addition to indenting and syntax highlighting. Integrated Development Environment is also known as Integrated Debugging Environment that offers you some facilities for developing software applications. An IDE consists of a source code editor, a compiler interpreter, automation tools and debugger.

The source code editor is designed to edit the source code of the computer programs. It simplifies the process of inputting the source code by auto completing and bracket matching functionalities. Build automation helps to compile source code into binary code. It runs tests and creates release notes. The debugger is used to test and debug other programs. It offers some sophisticated functions like running a program step by step and pausing the program to examine the present state. When you are just getting started it is essential that you learn the basics of computer programming. This will enable you to gain a solid foundation upon which to build your knowledge and experience.

LOGIC: BASIS OF COMPUTER PROGRAMMING

A computer program, as we have seen, is a set of instructions that we issue to a computer for it to carry out a task for us. To be able to tell the computer what to do, we need to have the basic idea or steps involved in our mind that would be required to complete our task.

This brings us to the concept of "logic", which in fact is the base and core of every computer program that you write - however simple or however complex the program might be. The logic, in simple terms, could be seen as the "trick" behind the solution to a problem. It is that instruction or set of steps that form the most important part of the program and is the basis of problem solving.

Consider for example - finding the average of 5 numbers input by a user. What is the first thought that crosses your mind when you think of the solution of this problem? Simple mathematics tells you, we need to add the numbers and divide them by 5. This very step, which forms the core to the solution of this problem, is in fact the "logic" behind the solution of this task and what our program would be based upon.

When we write a program for the above task, we will

1. Take the 5 numbers from the user

2. Add them

3. Divide them by 5

4. Give the result back to the user

Out of all these steps, as we can clearly see, the most pertinent steps depend on our entire output and the action the program performs are 2 and 3 - adding the 5 numbers and dividing them by 5. If we were to change these steps, the whole purpose and behavior of the program would change.

Consider for a moment that we replace steps 2 and 3 by the following:

1.   Take the 5 numbers from the user

2.   Take the first number and store it in a variable "SMALLEST"

3.   Take next number

4.   Compare with "SMALLEST"

5.   If number < "SMALLEST" then, store this number to "SMALLEST"

6.   Repeat step 3 to 5 for all remaining 4 numbers

7.   Give the result stored in "SMALLEST" back to the user

What do you notice here? The first and last steps are still the same. What we have changed is the core or the "logic" of the program, i.e. once the user has input the 5 numbers; we have changed what we do with the numbers!

This change now gives us the smallest number from the 5 numbers input as the result. This thus becomes a program to find the smallest number from a list of given numbers.

PROGRAMMING LANGUAGES TO LEARN

One of the most common questions we hear from individuals hoping to enter the IT industry is, "What programming languages do I need to know?" Obviously, this is a complex question, and the answer will depend on what field the questioner is going into. However, those already in IT know that the greatest skill you can have is to be a jack-of-all-trades. A well-prepared worker can switch between computer programming jobs with only minimal training, thanks to a wide knowledge of multiple programming languages.

Because of this, the quick answer to this question is, "As many languages as you can learn." Of course, if we took the time to learn every programming language possible, we'd never actually earn an income! This list covers essential computer programming languages a person trying to enter IT should know.

1.   HTML, CSS, and JavaScript

These three different languages are listed together because between them they make up the vast majority of website coding. Since the internet is now the dominant means of global communication, there will always be jobs in web design and development. HTML, CSS, and JavaScript are similar in many ways, but each has a different capacity to improve website function.

HTML stands for Hyper Text Markup Language and is the basic language of websites. HTML is used to insert images, links, basic formatting, and content onto a webpage. It's one of the easiest and usually, the first programming language aspiring IT professionals learn.

CSS is a natural extension of HTML that introduces more features to a website. CSS, or Cascading Style Sheets, allows for complex websites with constant formatting, by making individual web pages call up a separate piece of code that determines elements on the page. This allows for cleaner coding and a separation of layout and content.

JavaScript allows for client-side interactivity on a webpage and is designed to blend seamlessly with HTML and CSS. Text boxes, buttons, and pop-up are all functions of JavaScript.

2.	Java

Java is similar in many ways to JavaScript but is in fact unrelated. It's an object-oriented language with many uses and is designed to be both intuitive and stable. Java's versatility and widespread use make it handy for developers, and it'd be nearly impossible to find a successful programmer who didn't know it like the back of his or her hand.

Java is most often seen in web applications, where it can run more advanced GUI's than JavaScript. Many online games run through Java. It is not a particularly fast or powerful language, but it can do practically anything and is almost universally understood across different machines and operating systems. Because of this, it's a programming language every IT worker should know.

3.   C and C++

These two languages are old classics still widely in use today. C was developed in the 1970's and originally meant for use in systems programming. However, it soon became popular for consumer software as well thanks to its efficiency and versatility.

C++ was designed as an expansion to C in 1983. It is

now one of the most popular of programming languages and can be used for nearly every application. As one of the best developed and powerful programming languages in use, it is essential for IT workers to know. If you can only learn one language, learn C++.

4.   PHP

PHP is a server-side language that allows for interactive web pages. It is designed to use tags, and can thus be integrated with the basic HTML of a page. This may sound similar to JavaScript, but the key difference is that JavaScript works solely on the client-side. There are many occasions where having the interaction go through the server is desirable, and that's where PHP really shines. PHP also works well with Java, making it easier to call Java methods in your code. Combined with its compatibility with many types of databases, it's easy to see why PHP should be in every programmer's arsenal.

HOW TO LEARN PROGRAMMING LANGUAGES

The languages above will generally be enough to start with as a beginner, but there are a few more that you may come across. Ruby, Perl, and Python are all commonly used in advanced projects, so if you have the time they're well worth looking into. And of course, specific assignments may require any one of the many programming languages out there.

Don't let yourself fall behind in this competitive industry. Brush up on your programming languages today.

CHAPTER SEVEN

THE MATH INVOLVED WITH PROGRAMMING

Mathematics is used everywhere in the world and it is the most used science on Earth at the moment. Fields like electrical engineering, mechanical engineering, physics, and much more will make an extensive use of it. Computer engineering also uses math quite often.

Math logic is used in a lot of fields, and that also includes computer programming. When it comes to the Venn diagrams, they are very useful in understanding how logic works, but they are not only helpful in that regard as they can be used in computer programming as well.

In computer science, calculations also play a very important role. For example, the text that you are writing or reading on your computer's screen has been formatted in a specific way. This is definitely something that requires calculations.

For developing graphics, there is a field of mathematics that's used extensively; geometry. For instance, the graphics screen has a lot of similarities with the coordinate plane. Just as you will get to see the points in this plane, you will see that the graphics screen will have pixels.

Even though there is a massive number of points that can be observed in any of the bounded parts of the plane and the pixels of the graphics screen are limited, the techniques of coordinate geometry are still successfully employed in order to have different figures drawn on the graphics screen.

Developing software is something that implies a lot of transformations. There are 2 of them which are very popular and they are known as "'pop and push transformations'". In computer programming, there is a lot of use of mathematics by the classical C language; in addition, there are a lot of commands in this language which will make use of math extensively.

WEB APPLICATION PROGRAMMING LANGUAGE

Among computer programming languages, there is no single application that does all the different things, in all the different ways, that programmers need. Because of the great number and diversity of programming tasks, choosing a web application programming language has become a critically important step.

Fortunately, there is continuing development in the field, and today the number of capable applications is expanding. Database-driven websites can now be built with such varied scripting languages as PHP, ASP.NET, JSP, Perl, and Cold Fusion, which fall into two main groups - proprietary and open-source. In the foregoing examples, all are open-source except the proprietary Cold Fusion and ASP.NET.

1.   PHP Pros and Cons

As an open-source application, PHP was developed (and continues to be developed) by an active, engaged, international community of users. This is a great example of strength in numbers. The strength of PHP, of course, is cost. It's free!

Because it is free, the open-source software, PHP can be compiled and "tweaked" for most any operating system. In fact, there are even pre-compiled versions available for the majority of operating systems, both commercial and freeware.

You can also relax a bit more with PHP, as you can count on it being updated and improved more often than other languages. In an open, collaborative and non-hierarchical environment, suggested improvements can be adopted quickly. Again, this is a strength that is derived from its open-source status.

PHP is a mature application, though younger than Perl. However, it does have a few weaknesses that may be minor annoyances to some, but deal-killers for other programmers. Its lack of event-based error handling means that your workflow may be interrupted by a sudden jump to a special error-handling section. Finally, its lack of case sensitivity for its function names will run afoul of many professionals' long-established work habits.

2.   ASP.NET = flexibility

ASP.NET is arguably the most flexible of the

programming tools, and "plays nice" with both scripting languages (VBScript, JScript, Perlscript, Python) and compiled ones (VB, C, Cobol, Smalltalk, Lisp). This flexibility is also apparent in the application's compatibility with such development environments as WebMatrix, VisualStudio.NET, Borland's Delphi and C++ Builder.

On the downside, ASP.NET is a memory hog and somewhat slower to execute than its competitors. For this kind of application, that can be a serious weakness - on the internet, it may be called upon to scale to thousands of users per second. Its memory usage can easily become problematic on your server.

3.   JSP (Java Server Pages)

JSP is an open-source scripting language supported by Oracle, so developers can use Oracle JDeveloper to create JSP pages. This can be accomplished without having to learn the Java language first, relieving you of the task of writing Java scripts. It is also extensible, allowing Java tag library developers to outfit it with simple tag handlers that use a new, simpler, cleaner tag extension Application Programming Interface (API).

JSP has integrated the JavaServer Pages Standard Tag Library (JSTL) expression language, and it now supports functions. This greatly eases the creation and maintenance of JSP pages.

The most significant disadvantage of JSP is that there is no XML-compliant version of JSP comments, forcing developers to use client-side, HTML/XML-style comments (or embed Java comments). Depending, once again, on your particular needs, this may or may not be sufficient reason to eschew the use of JSP.

4.   A shiny Perl

An open-source language that is both mature and powerful, Perl offers web developers about every tool they need to create dynamic web pages. Like other open-source languages, it benefits tremendously from ongoing development, and the support offered by its international community of users is second to none.

Perl is particularly good for creating single websites quickly, cleanly, and elegantly. If it has a major identifiable weakness, it is that it may be unnecessarily complicated. If you are not comfortable switching gears among a variety of syntaxes, it may not be the best tool for you.

5.   The real ColdFusion

Originally built by Allaire and then purchased by Macromedia, ColdFusion is now owned by Adobe. It is very easy to get started building websites with it, and you can deploy powerful web applications and services with less training - and in less time, using fewer lines of code - than with PHP and JSP.

ColdFusion is now at version 8, although many programmers are still using the various iterations of ColdFusion MX, variously known as ColdFusion MX 6, ColdFusion MX 6.1, ColdFusion MX 7, ColdFusion MX 7.0.1, ColdFusion MX 7.0.2, ColdFusion 7, ColdFusion 7.0.1, and ColdFusion 7.0.2. However, ColdFusion MX to ColdFusion 8 is a valid upgrade path. In fact, upgrading to ColdFusion 8 is supported for the two most recent previous major releases of the program.

ColdFusion supports most major databases, from Oracle and Sybase to Microsoft SQL Server and Access. With its own markup language (CFML) and tags to connect to the database, it is relatively easy to create forms and dynamic pages. It also has all the benefits of CGI for today's broad based developers. Its weaknesses are few, but expert users will caution that it is probably the most difficult to maintain.

CHAPTER EIGHT

ELEMENTS OF A PROGRAM SPECIFICATION

EACH PROGRAM SHOULD BE DEFINED IN TERMS OF:

1. Input Descriptions (to collect data or request an output) - command line interface, verbal, optical, or through some other screen interface. All inputs should include:

a. Name, alternate ID, program label, description.

b. Defined layout and examples.

c. Input transaction specifications, including default values and editing rules for data to be collected.

d. Messages; e.g., data validation, and general processing.

e. Panels (for screens).

f.   Relationship of inputs to outputs.

2.   Output Descriptions (to retrieve data) - Printed report, audio/video, or through some other screen interface. All outputs should include:

a.   Name, alternate ID, program label, description.

b.   Defined layout and examples.

c.   Panels (for screens), maps (for reports).

d. Messages; e.g., general processing and program specific information/warning/error messages.

3.   Data Structure Descriptions (data bases, files, records, and data elements). NOTE: Programmers should NOT be in the business of designing data bases as they will only do what is convenient for their application, not others (thereby missing the opportunity for a company to share and re-use data). Physical files should be defined by Data Base Administrators.

a.   All data structures should include Name, alternate ID, program label, and description. They should also include...

b.   Data Bases - organization, key(s), labels, volume/size, backup requirements, internal structure.

c.   Files (both primary and working) - organization, key(s), labels, volume/size, backup requirements, internal structure, file-to-file relationships.

d.   Records - form, length, key(s), contents, record-to-record relationships.

e.   Data Elements - class, justification, fill character, void state, mode, picture, label, size, precision, scale, validation rules. If generated data, rules for calculation. If group data, rules for assignment.

4.   Program Description

a.   Name, alternate ID, program label, description.

b.   Characteristics: required processing speed, memory requirements.

c.   Dependencies to other programs externally (e.g., batch job stream).

d. Dependencies to modules internally (e.g., DLLs, subroutines, etc.)

e. Functions to be performed with inputs, outputs, and data structures (create/update/reference).

f. Special processing rules (logic for processing)

g. Command language required to execute the program (e.g., command files, JCL, etc.)

h. Physical environment where the program will be executed.

i. Test plan and how to assemble test data.

j. The method of implementation - programming language(s) to be used, design techniques to be observed, tools to be used.

In-house software engineering standards complement any program specification (and should provide guidelines for writing the specification).

Such standards define "best practices" for design and conventions to be observed during programming.

As an aside, the objective of software engineering should be:

- Maintainability (easy to correct and update),
- Performance
- Design correctness (proof),
- International support (to accommodate languages and cultures),
- Integration (sharing and reusing code), and portability (platform independence).

Between the programming spec as listed above and a good set of programming standards, it becomes rather easy to implement any program, be it by hand or through the use of a generator. As a matter of policy, specifications should be written under the assumption that a program generator will be used. This forces us to be more precise in our specifications.

CHAPTER NINE

GAME PROGRAMMING

It is essential to have an understanding of all the basic concepts regarding programming. If you don't know how to program, I would recommend starting with Python. It is a wonderful language that takes away the low-level details for the programmer and allows them to focus on concepts. It is also a very fun language; I'm sure you'll love to program in it.

Once you have picked up a language and know how to program, you need to decide which language you want to program your games in. That really depends on the kind of stuff that you want to do: engine development or game development. Engine developers create the core of the game, the engine, the stuff those powers up the actual game. If you choose this route, you will have to deal with all the low-level details of programming. For this, you should pick up C or C++ since most of the engines are coded in these languages. You should also be disciplined in memory allocation/deallocation and code optimization techniques.

The other path is to actually code the games, using a previously coded engine. In this path, you will use an engine created by someone else and use it to make your own game. Usually, engines have bindings in some scripting language (like Python, Lua, or Ruby) and thus you can code the actual game in a scripting language. You can focus on the game design rather than other low-level details.

Obviously, you can choose to do both levels: code the engine as well as the actual game.

In the beginning, I think it's better for you to wait after you've made some games to decide which way you want to go. With your first few games, it's better to code the entire game on your own. You will learn a lot along the way, and will also be able to decide which way you want to go. The best way to learn and remember something is to struggle through it the first time. Don't take short cuts; you'll thank yourself later.

To make games, you need certain extra libraries. If you know how to program, you must know what libraries mean. They are extra patches of code that you can link with your own code. To make games, you will need libraries for graphics, event handling, networking, etc.

If you're using Python, Pygame is an excellent library for beginners that provides almost all this stuff. For C or C++, you have Allegro and SDL. A simple Google search will give you a list of game programming libraries for the language of your choice.

Start playing with the library you have chosen. Read its tutorials online. Learn how to make simple things like rectangles, circles, load images, etc. Try to make some animations. The fundamental concept behind building an animation is to draw the object, then draw another object of same dimensions on top of it with the background color and then draw the earlier object, with its coordinates displaced by the required amount. Of course, if you do this quickly, you will be able to cause an illusion of movement.

After that, make a simple game. Google for game loop structure, it will help you out in coding the game. After you have coded it, move on to a slightly complex game, like a game with 2 tanks fighting it out. You don't have to get cute with graphics, just use whatever royalty free images you can lay your hands on. Try cloning more arcade games. To make these, you will have to use something called a level editor, something that is used in almost every game.

After that, try your hand out at a game which uses some AI, like a Pacman clone or a top-view soccer game. Both of them can be implemented using an FSM (Finite State Machine), a concept used for AI in 80% of commercial games. Then try your hand out at a side-scroller platform game like a Mario clone.

CHAPTER TEN

PROPERTIES OF A GOOD COMPUTER PROGRAM

Today, many businesses require computers to ensure the smooth running of the business. Therefore, the computers should have programs that are user-friendly and easy to understand. A few things will tell if a program is good enough for business use.

1.   IS IT READABLE?

If the program is in writing that makes it easy for a user to understand and follow the logic, then it can be termed as good. It should also have a systematic arrangement that will make it easier to troubleshoot the computer if anything goes wrong.

2.   EFFICIENCY

Your program should save you time. For you to process instructions you will need time and it will certainly use up some memory. A good program is that which works with less processing time and a small amount of memory. This proves efficient as you realize less waste.

3.   FLEXIBILITY

A good program should be able to accommodate different platforms, without having to make major changes to coding and software. It is a common phenomenon today to see different platform changes. Therefore, having a portable program will not be effective if the user decides to change the operating system. When proper computer programming is executed, your system will be able to handle modification. This happens due to many reasons, like a change of administration. It should only have simple codes that facilitate different amendments needed over time.

4.   PROPER STRUCTURE

For a program to be developed, the major tasks that are required to run the different systems should be broken down. A developer can also develop them independently in order to accomplish the job assigned to them without having to rely on other subtasks.

5.   PROPER DOCUMENTATION

Every program has to have good documentation, especially if the author will not be around for long. This is so that the other person handling it will find it easy to comprehend.

GOOD PROGRAMMING HABITS

1.   Before sitting down to code, you must have a formal or a paper-napkin design of the solution to be coded. Never start coding without any design unless the code is a trivial one.

2.   Good code documentation is as important as good knowledge of a programming language. Write brief logic for each major block of your code as comments in source code file itself. It's good to mention creation and modification dates of your program along with why modification was required.

3.   Maintaining versions of your program is another important task. Some present-day programming tools already have a built-in version

management. Whenever you make any change to your program, they save its copy as.bak file.

My approach is to maintain 3 versions of a program. Say, I have a file program.c which is used by other project team members as well. I copy this file as program.c.old as a backup and make another copy as program.c.wrk where I do modifications. When modifications are successfully compiled, replace program.c with the .wrk file. You can also append a date or some explanation phrase to your program versions like program260505.c or programReadFnWrking.c.

4.   If your project contains multiple source files then maintain a README file stating the purpose of each source files, data files, intermediate and log files (if any). You may also mention the compilation and execution steps.

5.   Ever wondered why your IF statement is not working as it should? Maybe you are using single equal i.e. "=" instead of "==" in the condition check. A good approach is to write condition in reverse order. So, your condition should read something like this:

if (10==i).... So, if you put a single equal sign by mistake then it will be detected at compilation time only as an error.

6. While using loops and conditional statements, always first put closing braces with corresponding opening braces and then write the inner statements i.e.

1)   for(int i=0;i<10;i++)

2)   {

3)   printf("i=%dn",i);

4)   }

The numbers at the starting of each line indicate the sequence of writing loop code.

7. Avoid using magic numbers. For example, instead of writing

circleArea = 3.14 * pow(radius,2);

use following code:

#define PI 3.14

circleArea = PI * pow(radius,2);

8.   Use meaningful variable and function names. For example, instead of using 'r' use 'radius' to represent the radius of a circle. Similarly, function name 'calculateArea' is better than any cryptic short name. In a hurry, we may use short variable names but the time saved leads to double wastage of time later when you have to guess what that short variable name stands for.

9.   Using print statements for later debugging is a good habit. But, removing them when the final code is ready is, sometimes, a risky task. So, make a function that displays debugging information passed to it. When your final version is ready, simply comment the internals of this function so this requires changes only at one place.

10.   Once you are done with coding, start optimizing your code. Some of the variables you declared earlier may not be of use at this stage. Similarly, statements which are not loop dependent can be moved out of loop block. Sound knowledge of compiler can also help in optimizing the code further.

11.   With good knowledge of your operating system and hardware, you can improve the performance of your program in terms of resource requirements etc.

12.   Always indent your code for clarity and easy readability.

13.   You may also like the idea of organizing project files into various folders like SOURCE, HEADERS, MAKE, EXES, etc.

14.   Study the code written by others. This will bring to you new programming techniques and what approach they have followed for the task for which you have also coded.

15.   Last but not least, take backup of your source-code files so that your effort doesn't go waste if your hard-disk crashes or a similar mishappening occurs.

CONCLUSION

When it comes to programming, the one statement attributed to Confucius will always remain true – "I do and I understand". While sitting in a classroom and learning the ideal way to program is obviously helpful, reading about computer programming concepts and trying out the real thing are 2 different ways of doing the same thing. What do you do then to quickly get yourself up and running to working with code? Well, that's the easy part...

The web is filled with clutter and some of this clutter is code snippets. While this may seem to be a bad idea, especially with all the wrong snippets of code lying all over the web, by immersing yourself into this world it will give you plenty of ideas on how to solve programming challenges and get you up and running on some of the major programming languages, the most common being JavaScript. JavaScript is one of the easiest languages to learn and the net is filled with client-side web scripts that can be accessed by simply accessing any web page, right-clicking and selecting "view source code". Check out ways that other programmers have used to resolve a particular programming challenge or how to do a certain task.

Soliciting feedback from people who already have more knowledge about a computer programming language will also go a long way in helping you think along fresh lines, or think about old ideas in new ways. How though, do you solicit feedback? One way is to join a strong helpful community. These communities are all over the web. There you can learn the culture, best practices for a particular language, and you can have your questions answered by experts.

Another way is to pair with another programmer and learn the ropes. This is a fashionable practice that has gained respect through the rise of the agile development computer programming methodology where 2 people get to work together on a project. The potential value of pair programming is indisputably superior when compared to programming on your own.

Computer programming also requires following predefined steps if you are to avoid typing time-consuming and tedious code that will not do what it's supposed to do. Programmers start by prototyping their programs. This involves creating the program interface with all the windows, dialog boxes and pull-down menus without adding action to them.

The next step involves choosing a programming language that will be easiest to write the program. The last step is to create mock-up instructions known as "pseudo code" that describe exactly how the program will work. Pseudo code is thus a valuable tool that you can use to outline the structure of your program and spot flaws in your logic. So what are you waiting for? Go and find a programming language that best suits you and dive right in! You may be surprised at how much you can pick up in just one sitting.

87

PART TWO

LEARN PYTHON

INTRODUCTION

Programming is a very useful and rewarding skill. As a programmer, there are few better moments than when someone sees you using a program you lashed together in hopes of making your life easier and says, "That looks really useful". Most people have, at some point in their lives, desired to accomplish something on their computer or even cellular phone and yet, have been unable to do so due to a lack of knowledge about programming and programming languages. Programming and its associated languages are used to communicate to the computer a set of instructions that will produce a desired outcome. While there are a huge number of programming languages, many of them have similarities; this means that once you learn one language quite well, in most cases you will be able to pick up a new one fairly quickly. If you know and understand a programming language, then there is often a fair chance that you can write a program to accomplish any task yourself.

CHAPTER ONE

ALL ABOUT COMPUTER PROGRAMMING

Computer Programming refers to the science of writing programs for the computer to perform tasks for us and to produce the desired results in a form that is useful to society. A Program is a set of instructions to the computer in a specific order enabling it to perform a specific task or function to produce a desired output or result.

WHAT IS A PROGRAMMING LANGUAGE?

As we all know, communication is a two-way process. The objective is that both parties are able to understand each other. If one fails to communicate in a way the other can understand, it leads to a Communication Gap. A Programming Language is used to bridge the gap between users and computers and allow the two parties to communicate data and desires into useable results. Programmers communicate with the computer when they issue instructions and provide data to be processed as input. The computer then communicates with us by providing the desired result as output.

SETTING REALISTIC GOALS

One thing that all new programmers must come to terms with is the amount of time learning a programming language may take. Although when you have become an expert and have the ability to write many programs quickly, you must remember that many programs have taken whole teams of expert developers years to create. So it is important to understand that knowing a programming language or even several is not enough to write some of the more complex programs you may have seen. Don't look at this new hobby as a way to save yourself a lot of money, as writing your own version of most programs will be out of your reach, for now. However, learning a new language can be accomplished with the use of a simple search engine and practice, practice, practice. Once you acquire a strong knowledge base a simple program could take you just ten minutes to write, but it may take thousands of hours to obtain a mastery level of the craft.

SELECTING YOUR FIRST LANGUAGE

Now that we have examined the limitations and handled some of the more unrealistic expectations, those of you still desiring to learn programming will be happy to know that it is not a hard thing to begin... It also does not require you to pay out huge sums of money. If you are reading this book online, you already have the resources to begin! Let us consider what your first language ought to be.

Traditionally, you begin with either Visual Basic or Python. The first thing to understand is that these two languages are very different. The simplest difference is price. Python is totally free; you can start writing Python now with just a text editor on your computer, though if you are on Windows, you will probably need to install it first. Visual Basic, often abbreviated to VB, is both free and not free. The version of Visual Basic newcomers learn is usually Visual Basic 6, but this is rather outdated and has been discontinued. So these days the version learned is often Visual Basic.NET which can be considerably less simple for newcomers. Visual Basic can be simpler for newcomers to learn because it allows you to build the interfaces (the part of the program the user will see) by dragging and dropping the different parts much like you would in art applications.

Visual Basic.NET must be developed inside what we call an IDE (Integrated Development Environment); this is basically a special program you use to write other programs. They also exist for Python, but their use is totally optional. The free Visual Basic.NET IDE is called Visual Studio Express. Regretfully, the full paid version of the IDE is not cheap and probably not appropriate for a hobbyist, but fortunately, to learn Visual Basic the free version is enough.

In practice, very few commercial programs are developed in Visual Basic these days, but the Visual Studio IDE allows you to use many other languages. The familiarity you will develop by using it will also allow you to use the power of the IDE for development in many other languages. Some will argue that almost every language can be developed in a text editor and that they are by far the most flexible way in which to code. While this is technically true (and I do suggest trying development in a text editor to compare once you get a little better), I would strongly advise learning your first language with a proper IDE.

While traditionally people learn Python or Visual Basic first and these are generally taught at schools, I am of the opinion that your first language should continue to be useful to you once it has served the purpose of helping you learn the fundamentals of programming. If I had to recommend one for newcomers, it would be Visual Basic.NET, as often the most complex part of programming is the graphical side of things and Visual Basic.NET utilizes simplicity through the drag and drop interface. These two languages are often used as introductions as they are very tolerant of mistakes and allow you to become confident in programming principles without worrying about more complex matters.

For those brave souls, I would suggest Java as your first language. Though it can be complex and is therefore not a common choice for a first language, it is very widespread and useful. Furthermore, it is very powerful and is available for free for both hobbyists and commercial uses. Java programs are different than most others in that they do not run on your computer. The user downloads Java and your code runs on what is called a VM (Virtual Machine). This means that your code runs in a special place Java sets up for it - a fake copy of your computer -

and handles the translation of this to the real machine for you. Java programs can be thought of as being a "cross-platform" meaning that they will, for the most part, run on Windows, Mac, Linux and most other operating systems.

Java is a good language to learn, however in contrast to Visual Basic and Python, it does not tolerate mistakes and requires you to be very specific about everything. It is also an object-oriented programming language. This is a very complex issue in which I will briefly try to summarize.

Languages like Python and Visual Basic are what is known as procedural languages, meaning that the lines of code are run one after another, Java is an object-oriented language and at the most basic level is all about objects. Object-oriented development is a term thrown around a lot these days in the programming world and while not always appropriate, it is generally considered a good idea. An object is an "instantiation" of a "class". A class is a blueprint used to describe something like a cat. The class contains both the data about the cat such as its name, age and owner as well as, "methods" which are essentially actions the cat can perform, such as meow or purr. An instance of the class "cat" would give you a particular cat. If you are brave enough to experiment with Java, you will come across this yourself in more detail. It is worth noting that Visual Basic.NET and Python both have support for object-oriented development and Java has the potential to be used procedurally, but these are not the languages' primary intended uses and are not often used. If you did not understand that comparison, don't worry about it too much. Object orientation is hard to wrap your head around, but any basic Java or another object-oriented language tutorial should help you understand everything in that paragraph.

A final reason Java is a good first language is that it is similar, in many ways, to JavaScript, which a scripting language as is Python. It is an entirely different class of language and learning Java will mean you understand JavaScript reasonably well. The differences between scripting languages and normal programming languages are that scripts are largely used for automated tasks while programs are used interactively by users. This is not totally true, as both types of languages are used for both tasks and most web programs are built in JavaScript, but does represent a broad generalization about the uses of programming language.

As for the actual language you pick, it is entirely up to you! Some may choose the traditional beginner language, some may explore all before making the final selection, and some may experiment with Java. Some of you may already have your eye on a language or fancy one of the more specialist languages like Scheme or Prolog. Whatever your choice, the path to mastery is the same.

IDEs

Many of the purists say that IDEs are a bad idea and are packed with unnecessary tools and menus that take up disk space while requiring a large amount of time to learn. While there is some truth to this, I feel that an IDE is definitely worthwhile. An IDE, integrated development environment, is a programming environment that has been packaged as an application program, typically consisting of a code editor, a compiler, a debugger, and a graphical user interface (GUI) builder. Many people offer free IDEs, such as Eclipse and Netbeans, for the more popular languages. There is also Visual Studio, which I mentioned previously. It is very intuitive, very powerful, and it supports many languages (much as

Netbeans and Eclipse do). If you chose to use Java, I would suggest Netbeans, as there is a packaged version of Netbeans with the JDK (Java Development Kit). Most languages need an SDK (Software Development Kit) to work with them and getting it installed properly as well as linked to the IDE is often the hardest part of the procedure. Visual Studio already comes with the development kits set up, which makes life easier, but other languages like Java and Python can be quite hard to set up properly. This is why I suggested the Netbeans + JDK bundle for those experimenting with Java, as it handles the complex set up for you, which will save you hours of suffering.

There are, in my opinion, three major advantages to using a fully featured IDE. First, they are usually extensible, meaning that there are many free plug-ins that could make your life a lot easier when you get a little more advanced. Second, and most importantly, is the ease with which an IDE allows you to debug your code. Most IDEs let you set breakpoints in the code, which will make the program stop when it gets to that point and let you step through it line by line. In this way, you can examine the contents of all the variables at any time.

For those of you who do not know what a variable is, I will briefly explain. A variable is a bit like a train station locker. You ask for one big enough to hold what you want to store and if what you want to store is the right shape, it can be stored there. When you write a program, any data you want to store temporarily will be held in one of these until you are done with it.

As the old programming saying goes, if you have not found any bugs, you are not looking hard enough. Almost no non-trivial program will work the first time and trying to work out where the problem lies, without the use of a debugger, is a pain I would not wish on anyone. Finally, an IDE will often give you advice on how to fix issues in the code. This can be very useful for fixing bugs and saves you lots of time searching the web.

LEARNING THE LANGUAGE

Now that you have a language and an IDE, it is finally time to learn the language. This, as you may or may not be surprised to learn, is not complex at all; it is simply time-consuming. To learn programming for the first time, there is no better way than exploration.

The key to learning programming is to have a goal. Think of a task, such as a system to keep track of where you are in all the various TV shows you watch, or a system to let you look at all the books you own in a particular category, or, if you feel brave, try to replicate part of something that you use on a regular basis. My advice would be to start small; perhaps make a sequence of message boxes that insults the user or a really simple calculator.

It is important when you first start that your goals are interesting, challenging, and entertaining. If you try to make really boring programs you will quickly get disheartened, so try to inject some comedy into your program. The calculator is a very good introductory program, but after you get a general idea it is important to set quite ambitious goals, because if you keep doing simple things you will never learn anything new.

It is important to try to incorporate some of the knowledge you have gained from previous work. One of the reasons most books fail to teach programming well is that they use small examples for each idea they introduce, whereas what you really need to do is plan the task without considering what you will need to accomplish it. This means you will be able to code some of it using what you already know, but most importantly, you will have to problem solve the part you don't. The best way to learn is to learn by doing. Go for a full program that does a task you wanted to do on a computer in the past, work on it, and when you are finished you will have learned a lot and you will have a useful (or at least entertaining) program, which is far better than some toy program demonstrating lists.

I have said that you learn by choosing to do projects where you are unable to do certain sections, thus requiring you to learn, but how do you go about finding out how to do them? It's simple and most likely the way you found this book.

Go to your favorite search engine (like Google) and search for what you want to do - for example: search "drop down list Java" to find some examples of using the drop down lists in Java. Because you will need it for another task, and not just to re-do the same thing the examples did, you will have to play with the examples you find and try to get them to do what you want. Just search each bit you need and before long you will find that most of the basics are as natural as waking up in the morning. As a bonus you will have done it all without spending a small fortune on books, without getting bored, and hopefully while being entertained. To this day, if I am bored, I sometimes break out one of my very first programs, which is just a list of boxes and a random number generators. It is your task to try to fill all the boxes such that the numbers the random number generator gives you are in ascending order; if you don't leave space and can't fit a number in a hole then you lose and must start again.

Once you have a few decent sized programs under your belt, you will find that you know the language well. You will also find that it is rare, no matter how well you know a language, to be able to write a program without resorting to Google, at least once, just to check something. So with that in mind, it could be argued that you learned the language without ever actually trying to learn it. Clearly, there are standards and good practices that you may not pick up on your own, but as you see more examples and read the comments you will find you adopt your own standards rather quickly.

LEARNING ANOTHER LANGUAGE

Once you have learned one language, whatever it may be, the most valuable thing you will have learned is all the key words for searches. When you want to do something in a new language, you need only search what you want to do and the language name. However, by now you will know the names used to refer to what you want to do, allowing your searches to be more effective and yield examples and answers much more quickly. As the fundamentals of programming are mostly the same, regardless of the language you use, you will be able to guess at the meaning of most of the code much more effectively once you locate an example. This will allow you to pick up most of the language very quickly.

If you take nothing else away from this chapter, remember that the best way to learn a skill is practice, practice, and practice some more.

Remember that programming is not something that can be learned overnight, and that to become a passable expert you probably need to spend at least 1,000 hours programming, so you will need to find ways to remain motivated. Break this into small chunks, and it isn't as much as you think. Don't think of it as learning to program rather, just start programming. Before you know it, you will be an expert. Programming is a skill, and while it is quite simple once you have the feel of it, it can be quite daunting to see your little calculator that took you a week and then consider what it takes to build a modern game.

Programming is easy when you know how, but it is important to set yourself tasks. These tasks should be interesting and, better yet entertaining, as they will be what keeps you programming and learning more and more until, one day, you wake up to realize that you have it! You are your own best tutor and the key is simply to jump in and get started.

CHAPTER TWO

WHAT IS PYTHON?

The Python programming language is a modern web programming language that was originally conceived and developed by Guido van Rossum in the 1980's. Since that time, Python has evolved into a high-performance programming language that is modular and extensible. Some of the largest websites in the world are utilizing Python, such as YouTube, Disqus, and Reddit. Python offers a number of features that make it an attractive programming platform including stability, portability, object-oriented development, a powerful standard library, and a wealth of third-party modules or packages.

WHY PYTHON?

1.   STABILITY

Python has been under active development since the late 1980's and is considered a mature programming language. The developers of the

Python language conduct extensive functionality and regression testing to ensure the language remains bug-free and stable with each new release.

2.   PORTABILITY

Python programming offers a number of features that make it an attractive option for web application development. Python applications are portable due to the fact that Python interpreters are available for all modern operating systems and some embedded computing systems.

3.   OBJECT-ORIENTED DEVELOPMENT

The object-oriented nature of Python makes it an ideal first language for new programmers and easy to learn for programmers migrating to Python from other object-oriented languages. Python programming is intuitive and reinforces good program structure and object-oriented methodologies.

4.   STANDARD LIBRARY

The standard Python library offers developers a plethora of features comparable to more complex languages such as C++ while maintaining simple and approachable language syntax. Comprehensive file-based I/O, database interactivity, advanced exception handling and a host of built in data types make Python appropriate for both web applications and general purpose programming. This makes Python web programming an easy task for application developers seeking to transition to web application development.

5.   THIRD PARTY MODULES

Python is known for being a comprehensive language with extensive functionality included in the standard library. However, the growing popularity of Python programming has led to a vast array of third-party packages, or modules, that extend Python's functionality and allow the language to deal with unique programming challenges. For example, modules are available for handling non-standard database interactions and advanced cryptography functionality. There are also modules available for dealing with common tasks such as reading file metadata, rendering charts, and compiling Python applications into standardized executable applications. Python web programming is made easier due to the availability of many web-centric modules to handle tasks such as e-mail, maintaining

HTTP state, interacting with JavaScript, and other common web development tasks.

ADVANTAGES OFFERED BY PYTHON

Python happens to be an easy programming language which offers its support to various application types starting from education to scientific computing to web development. Tech giants like Google along with Instagram have also made use of Python and its popularity continues to rise.

DISCUSSED BELOW ARE SOME OF THE ADVANTAGES OFFERED BY PYTHON:

1. FIRST STEPS IN THE WORLD OF PROGRAMMING

Aspiring programmers can use Python to enter the programming world. Like several other programming languages such as Ruby, Perl, JavaScript, C#, C++, etc., Python is also an object oriented programming language. People who have a thorough knowledge of Python can easily adapt to other environments. It is always recommended to acquire working knowledge, so as to become aware of the methodologies that are used across different applications.

2. SIMPLE AND EASY TO UNDERSTAND AND CODE

Many people will agree to the fact that learning and understanding a programming language isn't that exciting as compared to a tense baseball game, but Python was specifically developed with newcomers in mind. Even to the eye of a layman, it will seem meaningful and easy to understand. Curly brackets and tiring variable declarations are not part of this programming language, thus making it a lot easier to learn.

3. GETTING INNOVATIVE

Python has helped in bringing the real world and computing a lot closer with its Raspberry Pi. This inexpensive, card-sized microcomputer helps tech enthusiasts to build various DIY stuff like video gaming consoles, remote controlled cars, and robots. Python is the programming language that powers this microcomputer. Aspirants can select from different DIY projects available online and enhance their skills and motivations by completing such projects.

4. PYTHON ALSO SUPPORTS WEB DEVELOPMENT

With its huge capabilities, Python is also a favorite among web developers to build various types of web applications. The web application framework, Django has been developed using Python and serves as the foundation for popular websites like *The Guardian*, *The NY Times*, *Pinterest*, and many more.

Python provides aspiring programmers a solid foundation with which they can branch out to different fields. Python programming training ensures that students are able to use this high potential programming language to the best of its capabilities in an exciting and fun way. Those who are keen to make a great career as software programmers are definite to find that Python will live up to their expectations.

REASONS FOR LEARNING PYTHON

Python programming supports numerous styles such as functional programming, imperative, and object-oriented styles. Here are the top five reasons why a computer programmer must learn the Python language:

1.   Ease of learning: Python has been created with the newcomer in mind. Completion of basic tasks requires less code in Python, compared to other languages. The codes are usually 3-5 times shorter than Java, and 5-10 times smaller than C++. Python codes are easily readable and, with a little bit of knowledge, new developers can learn a lot by just looking at the code.

2.   Highly preferred for web development: Python consists of an array of frameworks which are useful in designing a website. Among these frameworks, Django is the most popular one for Python development. Due to these frameworks, web designing with Python has immense flexibility. The number of websites online today is close to 1 billion, and with the ever-increasing scope for more, it is natural that Python programming will continue to be an important skill for web developers.

3.   Considered ideal for start-ups: Time and budget are vital constraints for any new product or service in a company, and more so if it is a start-up. One can create a product that differentiates itself

from the rest in any language. However, for quick development, less code, and little cost, Python is the ideal language here.

Python can easily scale up any complex application and can also be handled by a small team. Not only do you save resources, but you also get to develop applications in the right direction with Python.

4. Unlimited availability of resources and testing framework: Several resources for Python are available today and these are constantly being updated. As a result, it is very rare that a Python developer gets stuck. The vast standard library provides in-built functionalities. Its built in testing framework enables speedy workflows and less debugging time.

5. Increased growth and income potential: Today top IT companies such as Google, Yahoo, IBM, and Nokia make use of Python. Among all programming languages, it has had amazing growth over the last few years. It is clear that Python is a vital language for web-based programmers. More can be learned at a reputed Python training institute.

WHAT IS NEW IN PYTHON PROGRAMMING?

In todays workplace, Python training is an increasingly important part of a programmers education. As a dynamic language, whose design philosophy revolves around readability and conciseness, Python is a popular choice for use as a scripting language. Like other interpretative languages, it is more flexible than compiled languages and it can be used to tie disparate systems together. Indeed, Python is a versatile language with many applications in growing fields.

For example, Python is a popular programming language for educational software. Raspberry Pi, the single-board computer project for teaching students computer programming, uses Python as its primary programming language. In addition, much of the software for the One Laptop per Child XO is written in Python. At the other end of the educational spectrum, Python is also a very effective language for scientific computing and mathematical software for theoretical mathematics. As educational software development continues to grow, Python will become a more and more important language to know and understand.

In addition to educational software, Python is also a favored language for use in AI tasks. Because Python is a scripting language with rich text processing tools, module architecture, and syntax simplicity, it is a natural choice for applications involving natural language processing.

Programs like Wolfram Alpha and Siri are just beginning to penetrate the end-user market and many such programs yet to come will be written in Python.

Moreover, Python is often used as a scripting language for web applications. For example, Google has adopted Python as one of the available languages in its Google App Engine, a cloud computing platform for developing and hosting web applications. Python is also used as a framework for program communications between computers for web applications like Dropbox. As web application development is a fast-growing field, programmers would do well to acquire some Python training to keep their skills up-to-date.

Python is also quite useful as a modern scripting language similar to Perl, which can be used to tie disparate systems together. Because of this, Python is a standard component for many Linux and Unix based operating systems, and because Python is used extensively in the information security industry, it is an important tool for systems administrators to learn, as well as programmers.

Python is becoming an increasingly vital programming language. Due to its versatility, it has a wide variety of uses in many growing fields. Both programmers and systems administrators would do well to pick up some Python savvy in order to keep their skills up-to-date.

CHAPTER THREE

INSTALLING PYTHON

Different people with a wide range of backgrounds, ages, and educational levels are involved in Python development today. You can become one of them, no matter whether you are a student, a computer designer, a housewife, or a retiree. There is always a number of thorough instructions to make your introduction into the matter easier and your success more sustainable. You can find many of them on the Internet. Here you may just get acquainted with some starting points and stepping stones of the process.

THE FIRST STEPS

To begin, you will need to download the Python source and its code. For better source control, the development team applies the Subversion of the most updated modification of every file in the project. If you want to start Python development on Windows, you will also need to download Microsoft Studio 2008, or just its free version called Express. If you use UNIX-like systems (Mac, Linux or others), you will have to install some special tools through your package manager. To start running Python, you will need to identify the type of platform to be able to invoke the interpreter in different manners. After the process of complete installation is finished, you may start working.

WHAT DO YOU NEED TO KNOW?

Use PEP-7 and PEP-8 tools as useful guides for the Python code base to ensure you are on the same page with everybody else. Always test your work when you change the code. You may find appropriate tests for each module in the test directory. As many people are working together with you simultaneously, they can see your stages of development. So, consider code reviews and comments a helpful means for writing a better code. This will also help you to stay away from bugs.

The most interesting thing in the whole process of Python development is its new features. They should be available with the corresponding documentation and code explanations. Try to write as much useful information as is possible. Even if you don't feel comfortable with the Python documentation, there is always a person who will be able to help you with the format.

Always test new features before you get your work accepted. Creating a patch is the next step to make your feature available for the core development team. You may use the "diff" command in your Subversion to generate this patch.

Python development is an educating and rewarding experience, as well as a way to expand your knowledge while providing the community with a service.

CHAPTER FOUR

PYTHON VARIABLES

According to several websites, Python is one of the most popular coding languages. Along with being a high-level and general-purpose programming language, Python is also object-oriented and open source. At the same time, a good number of developers across the world have been making use of Python to create GUI applications, websites, and mobile apps. The differentiating factor that Python brings to the table is that it enables programmers to flesh out concepts by writing less quantity and more readable code. The developers can further take advantage of several Python frameworks to mitigate the time and effort required for building large and complex software applications.

The programming language is currently being used by a number of high-traffic websites including Google, Yahoo Groups, Yahoo Maps, Linux Weekly News, Shopzilla, and Web Therapy. Likewise, Python also finds great use for creating gaming, financial, scientific, and educational applications. However, developers still use different versions of the programming language. According to the usage statistics and market share data of Python posted on W3techs, currently, Python 2 is being used by 99.4% of websites, whereas Python 3 is being used by only 0.6% of websites. This is why it becomes essential for each programmer to understand the different versions of Python and its evolution.

HOW HAS PYTHON BEEN EVOLVING OVER THE YEARS?

1.   CONCEIVED AS A HOBBY PROGRAMMING PROJECT

Despite being one of the most popular coding languages, Python was originally conceived by Guido van Rossum as a hobby project in December 1989. As Van Rossum's office remained closed during Christmas, he was looking for a hobby project that would keep him occupied during the holidays. He planned to create an interpreter for a new scripting language and named the project, Python. Thus, Python was originally designed as a successor to the ABC programming language. After writing the interpreter, Van Rossum made the code public in February, 1991. At present, the open source programming language is being managed by the Python Software Foundation.

1.   Version 1 of Python

Python 1.0 was released in January, 1994. The major release included a number of new features and functional programming tools including lambda, filter, map, and reduce. The version 1.4 was released with several new features like keyword arguments, built-in support for complex numbers, and a basic form of data hiding. The major release was followed by two minor releases, version 1.5 in December, 1997 and version 1.6 in September, 2000. The version 1 of Python lacked the features offered by popular programming languages of the time, but the initial versions created a solid foundation for the development of a powerful and futuristic programming language.

2.   Version 2 of Python

In October, 2000, Python 2.0 was released with the new list comprehension feature and a garbage collection system. The syntax for the list comprehension feature was inspired by other functional programming languages like Haskell, but

Python 2.0, unlike Haskell, gave preference to alphabetic keywords over punctuation characters. Also, the garbage collection system effectuated collection of reference cycles. The major release was followed by several minor releases. These releases added a number of functionality to the programming language like support for nested scopes, and unification of Python's classes and types into a single hierarchy. The Python Software Foundation has already announced that there will be no Python 2.8, however they will provide support to version 2.7 of the programming language till 2020.

3.   Version 3 of Python

Python 3.0 was released in December 2008. It came with several new features and enhancements, along with a number of deprecated features. The deprecated features and backward incompatibility make version 3 of Python completely different from earlier versions. Many developers still use Python 2.6 and 2.7 to avail the features deprecated from the last major release, however the new features of Python 3 have made it more modern and more popular. Many developers even switched to version 3.0 of the programming language to avail these awesome features.

Python 3.0 replaced print statement with the built-in print () function while allowing programmers to use a custom separator between lines. Likewise, it simplified the rules of ordering comparison. If the operands are not organized in a natural and meaningful order, the ordering comparison operators can now raise a Type Error exception. The version 3 of the programming language further uses text and data instead of Unicode and 8-bit strings. While treating all code as Unicode by default, it represents binary data as encoded Unicode.

As Python 3 is backward incompatible, the programmers cannot access features like string exceptions, old-style classes, and implicit relative imports. The developers must also be familiar with changes made to syntax and APIs. They can use a tool called "2to3" to migrate their application from Python 2 to 3 smoothly. The tool highlights incompatibility and areas of concern through comments and warnings. The comments help programmers to make changes to the code and upgrade their existing applications to the latest version of the programming language.

4.   Latest Versions of Python

At present, programmers can choose either version 3.4.3 or 2.7.10 of Python. Python 2.7 enables developers to avail improved numeric handling and enhancements for the standard library. The version further makes it easier for developers to migrate to Python 3. On the other hand, Python 3.4 comes with several new features and library modules, security improvements, and Python implementation improvements. However, a number of features are deprecated in both Python API and programming language. The developers can still use Python 3.4 to avail support in the long run.

5.   Version 4 of Python

Python 4.0 is expected to be available in 2023 after the release of Python 3.9. It will come with features that will help programmers to switch from version 3 to 4, seamlessly. As they gain experience, the expert Python developers can take advantage of a number of backward compatible features to modernize their existing applications without putting in any extra time and effort. Despite this, the developers still have to wait many years to get a clear picture of Python 4.0 and they must monitor the latest releases to easily migrate to the version 4.0 of the popular coding language.

The version 2 and version 3 of Python are completely different from each other. Each programmer must understand the features of these distinct versions and compare their functionality based on specific needs of the project. Also, they need to check the version of Python that each framework supports. Each developer must take advantage of the latest version of Python to avail new features and long-term support.

CHAPTER FIVE

OBJECT-ORIENTED PROGRAMMING

OBJECT-ORIENTED PROGRAMMING GENERAL CONCEPTS

The programming style that we usually call object-oriented programming (OOP) has appeared relatively recently in the history of programming languages. This is a particular and very convenient style for many situations. It was designed to overcome the limits of structured programming based mainly on the widespread use of procedures, functions, pointers, or other more or less developed data types.

Although structured programming is very practical for small software systems or reduced non-graphic applications, it should be avoided when dealing with large applications that use graphic elements where object-oriented programming is recommended. Object orientation means organizing software resources as a collection of distinct and discrete objects, which includes both data structures and their processing functions. This organization is an extension of structured programming in which the data structures and processing functions are only loosely connected. All items have their own identity and are perfectly distinct.

• An object is defined as an abstract concept, a specific and useful element for any application. Objects serve two specific purposes:

1. They provide a better understanding of the problem to be solved.

2. They provide a base design for implementation.

A class of objects encapsulates a certain number of objects with similar properties. This similarity refers to both the description (data and attributes) and the behavior (functions or methods). Attributes are unique features within an object class. Each attribute receives a certain value which can be modified during the object's life cycle. Two or more objects can have the same or different values for the same attribute.

Methods or operations are processing functions

applied to objects of a certain class. All objects within a class admit the same set of methods; methods which, in return, may receive any number of additional parameters.

In order to apply various methods to an object, it has to be created (defined). Defining an object is called instantiation. Once an object has fulfilled its mission it is removed.

Abstraction is a fundamental human trait that allows us to build models and thus cope with complexity. In every field of human activity, project approach is based on building a model for a better understanding of the problem to solve. Software engineering makes no exception. Through abstraction, the essential key aspects are isolated from the non-essential ones, therefore each problem may have several adequate models.

In the software engineering industry, structured programming has made a big step forward defining three perspectives needed in order to properly address any application. These perspectives, also known as models, are the static model, the dynamic model, and the functional model.

There are currently several object-oriented methodologies used for analysis, design, and implementation of software resources. One of these modeling methodologies is the OMT (Object Modeling Technique). This method of modeling involves the planning of the various development stages and a graphical representation of objects and their relationships.

OBJECT-ORIENTED SYSTEM DEVELOPMENT

The major motivating factor in the invention of the object-oriented approach is to salvage some of the flaws encountered in the procedural approach. Developments in software technology continue to be dynamic. New tools and techniques are announced in quick succession. This has forced the software industry and software engineers to continuously look for new approaches to software design and development, which is becoming more and more critical in view of the increasing complexity of software systems, as well as the highly competitive nature of the industry. Software engineers have been trying various tools, methods, and procedures to control the process of software development in order to build high-quality software with improved productivity.

The object-oriented paradigm draws heavily on the general systems theory as a conceptual background. A system can be viewed as a collection of entities that interact together to accomplish certain objectives. Entities may represent physical objects such as equipment or people and abstract concepts such as data files and functions. In object-oriented analysis, the entities are called the objects.

As the name indicates, the object-oriented paradigm places greater emphasis on the objects that encapsulate data and procedures. They play the central role in all the stages of the software development and therefore, there exists a high degree of overlap and iteration between the stages. The entire development process becomes evolutionary in nature. Any graphical representation of the object-oriented version of the software development life cycle must take into account these two aspects of overlap and iteration. The result is a "fountain model" in place of the classical "water fall model".

Object-oriented analysis (OOA) refers to the methods of specifying requirements of the software in terms of real-world objects, their behavior, and their interactions. Object-oriented design (OOD) on the other hand, turns the software requirements into specifications for objects and derives class hierarchies from which the objects can be created. Finally, Object-oriented programming (OOP) refers to the implementation of the programs using objects, in an object-oriented programming language, such as C++.

OOA provides us with a simple, yet powerful mechanism for identifying objects, the building blocks of the software to be developed. The analysis is concerned with the decomposition of a problem into its component parts and establishing a logical model to describe the system functions.

Object-oriented design OOD is concerned with the mapping of objects in the problem space into objects in the solution space and creating an overall structure and computational model of the system. This stage normally uses the bottom-up approach to build the structure of the system and the top-down functional decomposition approach to design the class member functions that provide services. It is particularly important to construct structured hierarchies, to identify abstract classes, and to simplify the inner-object communications.

Reusability of classes from the previous designs, classification of the objects of subsystems, and determination of appropriate protocols are some of the considerations of the design stage.

OBJECT-ORIENTED DESIGN

Object-Oriented Design begins with an examination of the real world "things" that are part of the problem to be solved. These things (which we will call objects) are characterized individually, in terms of their attributes (transient state information) and behavior (functional process information). Each object maintains its own state and offers a set of services to other objects. Shared data areas are eliminated and objects communicate by message passing (e.g. parameters). Objects are independent entities that may readily be changed because all state and representation information is held within the object itself. Objects may be distributed and may execute either sequentially or in parallel.

Object-Oriented Design is not dependent on any specific implementation language. Problems are modeled using objects. Objects have:

1. Behavior (they do things)

2. State (which changes when they do things)

For example, a car is an object. It has stated: whether its engine is running; and it has a behavior: starting the car, which changes its state from "engine not running" to "engine running" The various terms related to object oriented design are Objects, Classes, Messages, Abstraction, Inheritance, and Polymorphism.

1. Objects: An object is an entity able to save a state (information) and which offers a number of operations (behavior) to either examine or affect this state. Hence, an object is characterized by a number of operations and a state which remembers the effect of those operations. All objects have a unique identification and are distinguishable.

2. Classes: In any system, there shall be a number of objects. Some of the objects may have common characteristics and we can group the objects according to these characteristics. This type of grouping is known as a class. Hence, a class is a set of objects that share a common structure and a common behavior.

3. Messages: Conceptually, objects

communicate by message passing. Messages consist of the identity of the target object, the name of the requested operation, and any other operation needed to perform the function.

4. Abstraction: In object-oriented design, complexity is managed using abstraction. Abstraction is the elimination of the irrelevant and the amplification of essentials. We can teach someone to drive any car using an abstraction. We amplify the essentials: we teach about the ignition and steering wheel, and we eliminate the details, such as details of the particular engine in this car or the way fuel is pumped to the engine.

5. Inheritance: Inheritance is the technique that is used to build new classes from existing ones and to build object oriented class hierarchies. You can build layers of classes derived from other classes.

6. Polymorphism: When we abstract just the interface of an operation and leave the implementation to subclasses it is called a polymorphic operation and the process is called polymorphism.

OBJECT-ORIENTED PROGRAMMING AS WEB PROGRAMMING

Web programming is an aspect of web site development and the role of the web programmer is just as significant as the web designer's role in the web design aspect web site development. Programming languages have developed from machine languages to low-level languages and then to a high-level language. The high-level language which is a language close to natural language (the language we speak) is written using certain approaches. Notable are the monolithic and structural programming approaches. With the monolithic style, you write a whole program in one single block. In the structured programming approach, a program is divided into blocks of codes called modules, with each module performing a specific task. BASIC, COBOL, PASCAL, C, and DBASE that ran on MS-DOS platform could be written using both approaches.

Following the revolution of the windows operating system, it became possible to write programs using a more advanced structured programming approach than the type used on the MS-DOS platform.

This is the Object-Oriented Programming (OOP) approach where a program is divided into classes and each class is subdivided into functions or methods with each function providing a specific service. C++ and Java are typical examples of Object-Oriented Programming (OOP) languages which were originally developed for non-web solutions.

As the preference for web applications grew more and more, according to the historical development of the internet and the historical development of web, the need to improve on scripting languages continued to rise and one of the ways they embarked on that journey was by making scripts object-oriented. Java applet and PHP (Hypertext Preprocessor) are examples of Object-Oriented Programming (OOP) languages for web solutions. PHP was originally on object-oriented, but it has been fully upgraded to an Object-Oriented Programming language (OOP) demonstrating the 3 pillars of Object-Oriented Programming (OOP) - Encapsulation, Inheritance, and Polymorphism. Thus, it is possible to write server-side scripts in an object-oriented fashion.

Object-Oriented Programming (OOP) structures program into classes and functions or methods. To use a class and access the services rendered by each function, you must create an instance of the class. When an instance is created, an object is produced which is held by an object variable. It is this object that will now be used to access each function and make use of its service. The syntax of class instantiation statement for object creation varies from language to language. In PHP, you use the new keyword. For instance, if you have a class with name customer and you want to instantiate it and use the object to access function select records () in the class, you go about it this way-

$cust = new Customer ();

$cust->select records ();

The first line created an instance of class customer and an object held by object variable $cust. The second line accesses the service provided by function select records () with the object variable $cust. Java too uses the new keyword for object creation, but the application of the keyword in C++ is different where it is used by a pointer variable during dynamic memory allocation.

I mentioned earlier the three pillars of Object-

Oriented Programming (OOP)-Encapsulation, Inheritance, and Polymorphism. They are the integral features of PHP. Encapsulation is the process of hiding all the details of an object that do not contribute to its essential characteristics. This is achieved by making all instance variables of a class private so that only the member functions of the class can access its private instance variables.

Inheritance is a situation in which a class derives a set of attributes and related behavior from a parent class. The parent class is called the super class or base class and the inheriting class is called the sub class. The member variables of the super class become member variables of the sub class (derived class). In PHP, you use the keyword extends to implement inheritance just like Java.

CLASS CUSTOMER EXTENDS PRODUCTS

Polymorphism is an extension of inheritance. It is a situation when a sub class overrides a function in the super class. When a function or method is overridden, the name and the signature of the function in the super class are retained by the overriding function in the sub class, but there is a change in the function code.

Another important feature of Object-Oriented Programming (OOP) language is a constructor. A constructor is a function or method bearing the same name as its class name. It is used for initialization of member variables and invoked as soon as the class is instantiated, unlike other member functions that are invoked only with the use of the object variable. At this point, let us use submission of data with, for instance, fixed asset register form for further illustration. Your PHP script needs to retrieve data posted from the form, connect to the database, print custom error messages, and insert data into the database table. Using the Object-Oriented Programming (OOP) approach, you need 4 functions in the class-

The constructor to retrieve the posted data from the form.

A function to connect to MySQL database.

A function to insert a record into the database using the INSERT SQL statement.

A function to print custom error messages.

Because your program is in an organized form, it is

easier to understand and debug. This will be highly appreciated when dealing with long and complex scripts like those incorporating basic stock-broking principles. Within the limit of the structured programming capabilities of the non Object-Oriented Programming languages of BASIC, COBOL, PASCAL etc., you could organize programs by dividing it into smaller, manageable modules. However, they lack the encapsulation, inheritance, and polymorphism capabilities of Object-Oriented Programming (OOP) which demonstrates a great advantage of the Object-Oriented Programming (OOP) approach.

PYTHON TECHNOLOGY

Python is a dynamic and object-oriented programming language, widely used for web application development with 90% of people preferring Python over other technology because of its simplicity, reliability, and easy interfacing. It offers both powerful scripting and fast application development process across a vast range of fields. As the basis of several open-source platforms, Python supports with tools that help to build applications with excellent security and performance levels. Python follows procedural and object-oriented coding paradigms and hence, the varied applications that are written in Python come out with clean and readable code, making them easy to maintain.

USES OF PYTHON TECHNOLOGY FOR APPLICATION DEVELOPMENT

Python is an open source programming language, which is widely used in a number of application domains. It can perform on almost all operating systems like Windows, Linux, UNIX, OS/2, Mac, and Amiga. The dedicated Python Development team has written several applications based on Python programming language. Python is a fun and dynamic language used by a number of companies such as Google, Yahoo, and IBM. It is also used widely to write custom tools and scripts for special applications.

Python is extensively used in Web applications development such as Django, Pylons, and Games Applications like Eve Online, Image Applications, Science and Education Applications, Software Development, Network Programming, Mobile Applications, Audio/Video Applications, etc.

Python can be easily interfaced with C/ObjC/Java/Fortran. The key features of Python are its natural expression of procedural code, sound introspection capabilities, precision, readable syntax, instinctive object orientation, dynamic data types, extensions and modules easily written in C, C++, extensive standard libraries and full modularity, exception-based error handling, and it is embeddable within applications as a scripting interface. Python also supports the Internet Communications Engine (ICE) and several other integration technologies.

As a dynamic, general purpose programming language, Python is finding extensive usage by Python Development Services providers across the world for developing a wide range of software applications. It allows developers to express a concept with less quantity and more readable code. It enables the developers to integrate Python with varied other well-known programming languages and tools flawlessly.

Frequently the Python developers have the necessity to use diverse frameworks and tools to create high-end quality software applications within a short period of time. With the support of the resources offered by the varied Python frameworks, Python developers build sophisticated applications with minimal time and effort. Also, Python developers have an option to select from a number of Python frameworks such as Kivy, Qt, PyGUI, WxPython, Django, Flask, Pyramid, etc., depending on the nature and requirements of individual application building projects.

Python is a popular choice for use as a scripting language for many software development processes. Similar to many other interpretative languages, Python offers more flexibility than compiled languages and it can be efficiently used to integrate disparate systems together. Certainly, Python is a versatile programming language with several applications that are used in diverse fields.

THE FUTURE OF OBJECT-ORIENTED PROGRAMMING

The object-oriented paradigm is based on the idea that objects exist independently of each other and that operation can be executed on them. Consequently, a user in a true object-oriented development environment should be able to interactively create objects of any available class, manipulate these objects, and call their interface routines. Platform independence - "Write once - run anywhere" capability.

As a matter of fact, you cannot run a java program "anywhere", unless there is a virtual machine, but it's as good as anywhere. I know some folks who would say it's "write once debug everywhere", but any such platform dependent bugs are probably VM issues. All in all this platform independence is a huge plus point for enterprise development saving tons of cash and effort in porting products.

KEY FEATURES OF PLATFORM INDEPENDENCE

1. EASE OF USE

I'm not really sure how many hard nut programmers would agree with me, but programs are easy to visualize when they are object-oriented (once you get the hang of it). After the concept is built, it becomes much easier to realize it in code.

2. FREE RUNTIME/COMPILERS/TOOLS

This was one of the best moves by Sun. The runtime is free, the development kit is free, and now there are a ton of other tools built with java for java that are free. This makes Java development easy and affordable.

There are a number of ways to measure the popularity of a programming language, for example, based on the number of:

• New applications that are written in the language

• Existing applications that are written in the language

• Developers that use the language primarily

• Developers that use the language ever

• Web searches

• Available jobs that require skills in the language

• Developers' favorites

3. LOW COST

The tools needed to build and test Java programs are available without charge. Sun makes the Java Development Kit (JDK) available over the Internet, where faculty and students alike can download it. The JDK, which includes the Java compiler and interpreter, among other tools,is admittedly

Spartan, but students should find it adequate for most programming assignments.

Those willing to spend a little money will find nicer program development environments (such as Symantec Café and Microsoft J++) available at moderate prices.

4. EASY TO TEST

Students can put their programs, written as applets, on their Web pages for instructors to test and critique. Instructors can monitor a student's progress at any stage by simply visiting the student's Web page.

5. STUDENT ENTHUSIASM

Java has gotten so much publicity that students are bound to be excited about learning it. By harnessing that enthusiasm, instructors can use Java as a vehicle to teach students a tremendous amount about modern-day computing. Students will be motivated by Java's growing importance in the "real world." Moreover, students will be thrilled by the ease with which they can build sophisticated GUI programs.

6. SUITABLE FOR ADVANCED COURSES

After students gain familiarity with the basic features of Java in CS1, they can use its advanced features in later courses. For example, a course on operating systems can take advantage of Java's support for threads. The network classes that come with Java make it ideal for a networking course.

7. EASY TRANSITION TO C++ AND OTHER LANGUAGES

Java's syntactic similarity to C and C++ should ease the transition to those languages.

8. INTERNATIONAL APPEAL

The Unicode character set is an integral part of Java, allowing students to learn about the issues of developing software for the international market.

Java has significant advantages not only as a commercial language, but also as a teaching language. It allows students to learn object-oriented programming without exposing them to the complexity of C++.

CHAPTER SIX

WHY PYTHON?

As stated previously, Python was originally conceived by Van Rossum as a hobby language in December 1989. The major and backward-incompatible version of the general-purpose programming language was released in December, 2008. Python was recently rated by a number of surveyors as the most popular coding language. The massive popularity indicates Python's effectiveness as a modern programming language. At the same time, Python 3 is currently used by developers across the world for creating a variety of desktop GUI, web and mobile applications. There are also a number of reasons why the huge popularity and market share of Python will remain intact over a longer period of time.

REASONS WHY THE MASSIVE POPULARITY OF PYTHON WILL REMAIN INTACT IN THE FUTURE

1. SUPPORTS MULTIPLE PROGRAMMING PARADIGMS

Good developers often take advantage of different programming paradigms to reduce the amount of time and effort required for developing large and complex applications. Like other modern programming languages, Python also supports a number of commonly used programming styles including object-oriented, functional, procedural, and imperative. It further features automatic memory management, along with a dynamic type system allowing programmers to use the language to effectuate development of large and complex software applications.

2. DOESN'T REQUIRE PROGRAMMERS TO WRITE LENGTHY CODE

Python is designed with a complete focus on code readability. So the programmers can create a readable code base that can be used by members of distributed teams. At the same time, the simple syntax of the programming language enables them to express concepts without writing long lines of code. This feature makes it easier for developers to create large and complex applications within a stipulated amount of time. As they can easily skip certain tasks required by other programming languages, it becomes easier for developers to maintain and update their applications.

3.   PROVIDES A COMPREHENSIVE STANDARD LIBRARY

Python further scores over other programming languages due to its extensive standard library. The programmers can use these libraries to accomplish a variety of tasks without writing long lines of code. The standard library of Python is designed with a large number of high-use programming tasks scripted into it. Thus, it helps programmers to accomplish tasks like string operations, development, implementation of web services, working with internet protocols, and handling operating system interfaces.

4.   EFFECTUATES WEB APPLICATION DEVELOPMENT

Python is designed as a general-purpose programming language and lacks built-in web development features, but the web developers use a variety of add-on modules to write modern web applications. While writing web applications in Python, programmers have the option to use several high-level web frameworks including Django, web2py, TurboGears, CubicWeb, and Reahl. These web frameworks help programmers to perform a number of operations without writing additional code, like database manipulation, URL routing, session storage and retrieval, and output template formatting. They can further use the web frameworks to protect the web application from cross-site scripting attacks, SQL injection, and cross-site request forgery.

5. FACILITATES DEVELOPMENT OF HIGH-QUALITY GUI, SCIENTIFIC, AND NUMERIC APPLICATIONS

Python is currently available on major operating systems like Windows, Mac OS X, Linux, and UNIX. The desktop GUI applications written in the programming language can be deployed on multiple platforms. The programmers can further speed up cross-platform desktop GUI application development using frameworks like Kivy, Wx Python, and PyGTK. A number of reports have highlighted that Python is used widely for the development of numeric and scientific applications. While writing scientific and numeric applications in Python, the developers can take advantage of tools like Scipy, Pandas, IPython, along with the Python

Imaging Library.

6.   SIMPLIFIES PROTOTYPING OF APPLICATIONS

Nowadays, each organization wants to beat the competition by developing software with distinct and innovative features. This is why prototyping has become an integral part of the modern software development life cycle. Before writing the code, developers have to create a prototype of the application to display its features and functionality to various stakeholders. As a simple and fast programming language, Python enables programmers to develop the final system without putting in any extra time and effort. The developers receive the option to start developing the system directly from the prototype simply by refactoring the code.

7.   CAN ALSO BE USED FOR MOBILE APP DEVELOPMENT

Frameworks like Kivy also make Python usable for developing mobile apps. As a library, Kivy can be used for creating both desktop and mobile applications. It allows developers to write the code once and deploy the same code on multiple platforms. Along with interfacing with the hardware of the mobile device, Kivy also comes with built-in camera adapters, modules to render and play videos, and modules to accept user input through multi-touch and gestures. Thus, programmers can use Kivy to create different versions of the same applications for iOS, Android, and Windows cellular phones... The framework does not require developers to write long lines of code while creating Kivy programs. After creating different versions of the mobile app, they can package the app separately for the individual app store. This option makes it easier for developers to create different versions of the mobile app without deploying separate developers.

8.   OPEN SOURCE

Despite being rated as the most popular coding language, Python is still available as open source and free software. Along with large IT companies, the startups and freelance software developers can use the programming language without paying any fees or royalties. Thus, Python makes it easier for businesses to significantly reduce development costs. The programmers can also avail the assistance of the large and active community to add out-of-box features to the software application.

CHAPTER SEVEN

HOW TO PROGRAM IN PYTHON

Python is a dynamic language and supports different programming styles, including object-oriented, aspect-oriented, functional, and imperative. One of the best features of the language is ease and enhanced memory management. Essentially employed as a scripting language, Python offers a great level of functionality. While it can be used as a stand-alone program, you can also integrate third party tools and customize its functionality.

One of the highlights of Python is that it is a highly extensible language. This means that various functional elements are not built into the core of this platform. Rather, you can use third-party applications and extend the platform's functionality. Additionally, you can integrate a Python code into an existing program and create an interface for programming. This is called Embedding and Extending.

As mentioned above, syntaxes of Python are simple.

Complicated syntaxes are rejected and the platform embraces codes that are less cluttered and sparse. This does not in any way influence the performance or functionality of programs. Also, unlike other popular programming languages such as Perl, Python does not offer unnecessary clutter by giving the programmer multiple ways of achieving the same purpose. Python's philosophy is to offer one powerful way of obtaining one result. This philosophy is the main driving force behind the simplicity of Python. So, if you want to become adept in this language, you need to change your mindset and think in a simple and straightforward manner. The simplistic approach towards programming works best with Python.

In order to aid simplicity, Python coding and syntaxes use English words rather than punctuations or symbols. This enhances the readability as well. Some examples of statements written in Python include "if", "for", "while", "try", "class", "def", "with", "yield", "import", and many others. Most of the commands used are self-explanatory.

Owing to the ease of handling, Python is a "programmer's language". Moreover, learning the language is very simple. One of the biggest advantages of Python, besides clear and easily readable codes, is the speed with which you can code. Programmers can go on the fast track because multiple levels, which are not necessary, can be skipped. Another advantage is that programmers get a lot of support from the Python open source developer community.

The portability feature of Python is another one of its major strengths. Not only can Python run on multiple platforms, but also programmers only need to write a single program to work on all operating systems such as Linux, Mac, Windows, and others. It is a highly adaptable language. Learning Python is not a tough task even for beginners, so take the leap and master Python!

CHAPTER EIGHT

TIPS FOR LEARNING TO CODE THE EASY WAY

Learning to code is one of the toughest decisions you can make. At first, we start with a very high enthusiasm and zeal to beat the beginner stage in 21 days or less, but all too soon we hit a brick wall and end up being novices.

Learning to program is like learning to speak a new language. Learning a few phrases of a foreign language doesn't make you fluent. The same applies to programming languages; learning new syntax doesn't make you a pro.

These disappointments caused by our eagerness to take the shorter way through can become burdensome. In these few steps, I will be providing with some cool tips for starting your programming journey and reaching your full potential.

1.   LEARN HOW YOU LEARN

Knowing how you learn not only helps you in programming, but in everyday life. First, understand your own personal learning pattern. I would suggest you relax and don't try to memorize codes. You will become fluent with time and practice. If you want to build a career with programming you should first relax and identify your learning curves. These include the best time of the day that your brain assimilates faster, the best environment for you to learn, and learning methods that are tailored to your own personality.

2.   KNOW WHERE TO START

It's important to know what programming language to learn and where exactly to start. It's a bit confusing when choosing a language to learn, especially if you do not have any special area of interest. Find a problem and a related programming language to solve that problem. For example, if you are trying to solve a problem with web technology, subscribe to learn Python and other web related programming languages. Read books and articles to learn about these languages before choosing which to learn.

Sometimes it's boring reading the introduction

when you pick up a book, but some information provided there could be helpful in the rest of the chapter. Also, read books and watch video tutorials to get started and become familiar with the basics. Growing a career and developing a working program requires practice!

Look for a new challenge around you and try to apply the basics you've learned. The more you are trying to figure out and solve the problem, the better you are at programming.

3.   GET HELP

Never try to do it on your own. Subscribe to tutorials online and offline. Go to seminars and programming group meetings. Meet other programmers, observe, and ask questions. Get mentors for guidance. It's easier learning with other programmers, so don't be intimidated by their skill. Be patient, observe, and learn! Even pros do not work alone. Subscribe to forums and websites like Stack Overflow, Github, Udemy, Cousera, etc.

4.   CHALLENGE YOURSELF AND KEEP AT IT

Challenge yourself to solve a real life problem,

especially a problem relating to you or something you are very passionate about. Re-solve the same problem you have already solved with an easier method (fewer lines of code or a new approach entirely). The more you look for new ways to solve problems, the better you will become.

Don't be tempted to jump into another project when you are faced with a challenge because chances are that you would keep jumping in and out of projects and languages and never get any work done or master a language. Keep practicing, even though working on the same project over and over again can be boring. I assure you the second or even third attempt will be easier with a consistent effort. A cool trick to staying on programming without burning out is, when you are not coding try to think about it, the more you think about it, the more your actions and body responses move towards it; keep a list and check things out daily.

5.   BE UPDATED

Always keep in touch with recent updates and upgrades. If you think you are good enough on a language or want to solve problems on other platforms, pick up another language and explore.

Never limit yourself, the more versatile you are, the more successful you will become. Subscribe to email listings and blogs that keep you updated.

CONCLUSION

The web is full of free resources that can turn you into a programmer. If you've always wanted to learn how to build software yourself or perhaps write an occasional script, but had no clue where to start, then continue to learn!

If you're interested in becoming a programmer, you can get off to a great start using tons of free web-based tutorials and resources. Since the early days of the Internet, programmer communities have been using it to discuss software development techniques, publish tutorials, and share code samples for others to learn from and use online.

A common issue for beginners is getting hung up on trying to figure out which programming language is best to learn first. There are a lot of opinions out there. In the end, language doesn't really matter. Understanding data, control structures, and design patterns are key. Every programming language, even basic scripting languages, will have elements that will make other languages easier to understand.

Many programmers never actually take accredited academic courses and are actually self-taught in every language throughout their careers. This is achieved by reusing concepts already known and referring to documentation and books to learn its syntax. Therefore, instead of getting stuck on what language to learn first, simply pick the kind of development you want to do and just get started using the one that comes the easiest to you.

There are several different kinds of software development you can do for various platforms; web development, desktop development, mobile device development, and command line. My opinion would be to learn Python because it is one of the most useful and widely adapted programming languages in the world.

PART THREE

PROCRASTINATION

INTRODUCTION

Procrastination is the habit of putting off or delaying an action or task to a much later time. This word was originated from the Latin pro, meaning "forward, forth or in favor of" and crastinus, meaning "of tomorrow". Procrastination is considered by many as a negative attitude and a counter-productive habit. With that being said, it is seldom viewed in a positive light.

However, procrastination's positive form, as the subsequent historical analysis specifies, is only secondary in usage. Like the rest of common-language terms outlined into scientific study, definitions for procrastination tend to be almost as abundant as the people researching this topic. At the outset, such variation in definition may seem to complicate the nature of procrastination; but in a way, it may also serve to partially illuminate it. Let me explain...

The different attempts by many researchers to refine the understanding of its meaning are more complementary rather than contradictory.

Moreover, any common idea only uncovers a core or essential element. It is obvious that all definitions and conceptualizations of procrastination identify that there must be a postponing, delaying or putting off of a task or decision, in keeping with the word's Latin origins.

Based on this, a procrastinator is someone who delays starting or completing a course of action or task. This distinction is relevant, as there are hundreds of tasks that one could be doing at any time, and it becomes burdensome to think that one is putting them all off.

Procrastination nowadays is particularly widespread. Everybody seems to be inflicted with it. It is like a modern disease that knows no race, sex, age or boundary. Some of us may put off tasks every now and then; but for many, it is a way of life to them. In a more recent study, an estimate shows that 80%-95% of college students procrastinate and approximately 75% deem themselves procrastinators, where almost 50% describe themselves as chronic procrastinators.

The total amount of procrastination among students is substantial. It typically takes over one-third of their daily activities, often acted out through sleeping, playing games, social media browsing, or watching TV.

So why do so many people procrastinate? Are we just born this way? I believe the answer is a big NO. We become conditioned procrastinators. One of the reasons is that we fail to look at what causes procrastination. Those seeking to stop procrastination need to first identify the root causes. Only when you know the why, can you make the changes to overcome procrastination.

PROCRASTINATION STATISTICS

Figures on procrastination basically involve the use of statistics, normally utilized in organizations for gathering information on the number of procrastinating workers. This would help the organization to find the causes affecting their profits and the reasons as to why workers procrastinate. It is already well known that procrastination is a term which states the person will defer a task for a later period, which should have been performed at a current period. There are many reasons as to why people prefer to avoid these tasks, which we will cover later on.

Although a person can indulge in procrastination at any point in time, there are high probabilities of occurrence of procrastination at the approach of a deadline. More so, procrastination can also occur during odd moments as well. On some occasions, it may also happen even before a person understands why they're even procrastinating in the first place.

ROUGH ESTIMATIONS

Based on a few local studies, it is estimated that as much as 95% of people are prone to procrastination. Amongst them, 20% of them are chronic procrastinators (this study is separate from that of the college student survey earlier). These individuals have an increased chance of losing their jobs, having financial problems, and having serious problems in their relationship with others.

In addition, when experts do have statistics on procrastination at hand, they can formulate theories as to why a person embarks on this procrastination journey in the first place. Although, it is known that anxiety is the leading cause as to why people procrastinate, there are still many other reasons behind procrastination. It is essential to have a serious look at procrastination, as it affects both the individual and the organization where he or she works or studies.

CHAPTER ONE

WHAT IS PROCRASTINATION?

1.   PROCRASTINATION CAN BE DEFINED AS DEFERMENT OF ACTIONS OR TASKS TO A LATER TIME.

We can say fundamentally that procrastination is the act of putting off the essential task until a later time. Most of the time, non-essential tasks are done in lieu of the more critical ones.

Psychologists term such behavior as a mechanism for coping with the anxiety associated with starting and completing any task or decision.

Usually, the behavior of a person procrastinating is:

Counterproductive

Needless

Delaying

Issues concerning procrastination are anxiety, low

sense of self-worth, and a self-defeating mentality.

Procrastinators basically have a lower-than-normal level of conscientiousness.

The approach is mostly based on the "dreams and wishes" of perfection contrary to a realistic appreciation of their obligations and potential.

2.   PROCRASTINATION IS A HABIT, BUT THE GOOD NEWS IS - LIKE ANY OTHER HABIT, IT CAN BE BROKEN.

If unchecked this habit can have serious consequences on our life as well as the lives of the people who surround us.

Procrastination becomes dangerous if further unchecked as it can affect the mental and physical health of the individual.

Here are some suggestions to help you get started and stop procrastination:

Realize that the task to be done is to be done - there are no alternatives.

Self-reflection will help us to determine our personality and know why we are avoiding the particular task. Is it simply our self-defeating behavior or lack of knowledge? If so, learn the task and do it.

Use positive words instead of negatives, as words have meaning and they impact us.

Being confident of our information, equipment and time limit ensures that the task is done on time.

Making realistic expectations and prioritizing on the tasks keeps us well focused on the goals.

Motivation and rewards can self-help us in accomplishing the tasks efficiently.

Let us beat the habit of procrastination with a quote from Napoleon Hill - "Procrastination is the bad habit of putting off until the day after tomorrow what should have been done the day before yesterday."

COMMON CAUSES OF PROCRASTINATION

Most people would admit to having been plagued by procrastination at some point in their lives. A small amount of procrastination, if it only happens sometimes, is normal.

To some people though, procrastination is a cruel habit that prevents them from fulfilling their daily duties effectively, causing them to fail at achieving their career goals. Procrastination happens when there is a gap between when a person is supposed to do a task and when he or she actually does it.

When you find yourself dropping more important tasks in favor of an easier, less important one, then you are procrastinating. The reverse is not the same.

Choosing a more important task over a less important one may just fall under good prioritization. Knowing the causes of procrastination can help you fight this habit and avoid it from becoming a chronic condition for you.

CAUSES OF PROCRASTINATION

1.   LACK OF ORGANIZATIONAL SKILLS.

One of the most common among the causes of procrastination is a lack of organization skills. Most people procrastinate on a task because they have not figured out how important the task is. Organized people find it hard, if not impossible to procrastinate because they use such tools as To-Do lists that show how important tasks are relative to others.

They also have schedules that tell them when they need to start certain tasks in order to finish them on time.

2.   GETTING OVERWHELMED

Another cause is a feeling of being overwhelmed by a task and fear of success. This happens particularly when your boss gives you a big project without telling you how he or she wants it done. Your boss is leaving the details up to you because he or she trusts that you are equal to the job. Do not let your boss down.

To fight being overwhelmed, break down the project into small, manageable tasks. This will help you get started.

3.   FEAR OF SUCCESS

A fear of success may be causing you to procrastinate. If you are afraid of the consequences of successfully finishing a task, you might procrastinate on it. You may be afraid that you will be given more additional work if you succeed on this one, or maybe be reassigned to another department that needs your skills. Whatever it is, recognize that procrastination will not help further your career either.

4.   BEING A PERFECTIONIST

Another cause of procrastination is being a perfectionist. Perfectionists procrastinate because they dwell on the fact that the perfect circumstances for a perfect outcome do not yet exist. So, they put off a task because they cannot do it perfectly today, or they do not have the perfect resources. Surprisingly, perfectionists are imperfect this way.

5.   LACK OF DECISION-MAKING SKILLS

Lack of decision-making skills can also cause you to put off tasks. If you do not know what to do, you will put off doing it. An example is wanting to move to another job but not knowing what kind of job you want to move to. It will result in you procrastinating on sending in your applications.

Congratulations, you are now better-equipped to recognize and battle procrastination, now that you know the cause.

Procrastination is a very common problem that can lead to increased stress levels, lost opportunities, heightened frustration, and ultimate failure. To effectively overcome this problem and increase your chances of a more productive and successful life, you first need to understand the common causes of procrastination

REASONS WHY PROCRASTINATION ISN'T HEALTHY

1.   PERSONAL CIRCUMSTANCES

If you repeatedly set back household chores or relationship duties, such as pitching in with washing the dishes or cooking, disposing of and taking out the garbage, then your marriage life and other relationships may suffer. You may think it's a slippery slope, but these circumstances do in fact occur, sometimes on a daily basis.

2.   GIVES YOU NO INNER PEACE

Another reason why procrastination is bad is because it takes away your inner peace. You are always late for appointments or meetings; you are always hurrying out the door, applying makeup in your car, calling or texting while driving on the road, and in fact risking your life and of those around you. It may seem like an easy thing to postpone, such as dental appointments; however, the instant your cavity gets worse and you miss a day of work with your significant sales presentation, you drop that client and your expectations for a promotion, then you'll realize why procrastination is not good.

3.   HURTS YOUR RELIABILITY FACTOR

Yes, procrastination hurts your reliability and credibility. If your friend needs something from you, your character may be so tarnished that he or she may not rely on you in a time of need. Your best friend may have gotten sick and needs to pick up their kid from elementary school, however, they may possibly think twice before asking you for a favor because they know you may not punctual or will be indecisive until school is almost out. You may be thinking that's a good thing, but just keep that in mind for the next time you need a favor from them.

HOW TO OVERCOME PROCRASTINATION

There is no solution for procrastination except to take action. Taking the necessary action when required to is the only solution there is. Most people procrastinate when it's time to go to the gym or work out, but in fact report feeling better after going to the gym or exercising. Whenever you procrastinate, you are left feeling guilty and even depressed at times. People who lack the motivation to accomplish even minimal tasks have been found to be borderline depressed or manically depressed. You will always feel better after you get things done.

Procrastination adds to depression and can cause one to experience bad health, bad relationships, failing grades, and poor work performance which can lead to the loss of one's employment. No one wants to experience these things happening to them, so why do they procrastinate?

A.   RECOGNIZING PROCRASTINATION

The first step in overcoming procrastination is acknowledging that procrastination exists. You can't fix the issue until you first recognize that you have a problem. It's kind of like having a medical issue. You cannot get the needed treatment that's required until you first acknowledge and diagnose the issue, then you can move on to treating the problem.

The following are several symptoms and signs that will help you realize when you are procrastinating:

- You usually fill your day with low priority tasks.
- Reading e-mails over and over again without even knowing how to start working on them or what you should be doing with them.
- Skipping an item on your to-do list for a long period of time, although you know that it is important.
- Sitting down before your computer or your desk to start doing a high priority task and you almost instantly goes off to make a cup of tea or take your phone out.
- Regularly accepting unimportant tasks that others would like you to do, and you spend your time on these instead of working on with the important ones that are already on your list.
- Usually waiting for the right time or the right mood to do the essential task at hand.

B.   ESTABLISH WHY YOU PROCRASTINATE

Understanding the "why" behind your procrastination moves you closer to overcoming it. Let's say you are putting off cleaning your house. Maybe it's because you've allowed it to get so out of hand that it's become overwhelming to you and you just wish it would go away. Usually, procrastination takes place whenever a task that needs to be done is not pleasurable. Most humans have no problem with getting things done that's pleasurable to them. It's human nature. We are designed to move away from pain and draw close to pleasure.

- An unpleasant or boring job could sometimes be the reason for your procrastination because you try to avoid it. To resolve this, finish them quickly so that you can proceed and focus on the more pleasurable aspects of the task. Break this large task down into smaller tasks you can do back to back.
- Another reason could be because you are not organized. The best way to deal with this is to make and prioritize your own to-do lists and schedules.
- Perfectionists are usually procrastinators for they tend to think they do not have enough skills or resources to do the task perfectly, so they end up to not doing it at all.

4 EASY STEPS TO COUNTER PROCRASTINATION

1.   Mind shifting: since we recognize that humans are wired to move away from painful things, try associating procrastination with the consequences of not getting important things done. Create a mental picture of the negative results that can occur if you don't get things done. This mental shift can give you the motivation to take action in order to avoid the pain of the consequences.

2.   Prioritize: Sometimes you may procrastinate because it seems like there's so much to do yet so little time to get things done. A way to overcome this type of procrastination is through prioritizing. Write down a "to-do" list and then look it over to see what tasks are most important and what tasks are least important. Then prioritize those tasks according to their importance level (1 being the most important while 10 being the least important, or vice-versa) .

3.   Accountability Partner: Appointing someone to hold you accountable is another great way to combat procrastination. We usually attempt to do what we say when we know that someone else is watching us and will hold us accountable.

4.   Plan ahead: This step can tie into step 2. Establish your priority "to do" list the night before. Accomplishing your list ahead of time can, first of all, give you a boost of confidence since you've gotten something done. You may also find yourself sleeping better at night looking forward to the next day. Since we cannot predict with certainty the events of tomorrow, be prepared to change some things around on your list if need be.

Procrastination is a habit that is hard to kill. Here are helpful motivating factors for you to get moving forward:

• You need to make up your own rewards, like promising yourself some dessert if you have finished a certain task. Make sure you become aware of how good it feels to complete things.
• Peer pressure does really work. You may ask a friend or a co-worker to check up on you. This is said to be the principle behind self-help groups, and this is generally renowned as a highly effective approach.
• You should spot the consequences of not doing the chore.

CHAPTER TWO

WHY DO WE PROCRASTINATE?

How many times have you avoided cleaning your closet reasoning with yourself about other important tasks that you may have to do or convincing yourself how cleaning is not 'significant' enough to be completed at this point in time? Congratulations, for you, are procrastinating the task. And hey, welcome to the club. It must be good to hear that you are not the only one. Well, here's some more good news. There are millions of procrastinators all around the world. Scratch that – more like billions. Now it's time for the bad part. If not acted upon, then procrastination can very well affect your productivity, your efficiency and even your ability to function normally in your day to day life if it isn't already.

THE COMMON SYMPTOMS

A procrastinator often spends up more energy in putting off a task than what he or she would have spent in completing it. The mind gives constant reminders about the task and a person will try his or her best to put the thoughts away, often eating up one's own positive energy resource. Such thoughts can not only be an energy drainer but can also weigh down heavily on the confidence of a person. In simple terms, procrastination is nothing but self-sabotage.

TYPES OF PROCRASTINATORS

Here's some more juicy insight, such as the different types of procrastinators. The first category is relaxed procrastinators and the second is tense-afraid procrastinators. I think the names are pretty self-explanatory, but here's a detailed description.

• A tense-afraid procrastinator will usually avoid a task because he/she is too tense to handle the stress that the task may bring about. At times, he or she is confused about the importance of the task and is unable to prioritize these tasks in life. In most cases, this leads to further procrastination. For example, studying for an examination. He or she will be too worried about not being able to complete the studies and will, in turn, make frequent trips to the washroom, drink coffee, scroll through social media and end up delaying the actual task further.

- The relaxed procrastinator, on the other hand, avoids a task only because he or she doesn't care. They focus their energy on other more enjoyable tasks. A prime example in teens is when they procrastinate their studies but do not do the same with their social lives. It's just a matter of diverting the energy within the body to something more enjoyable, such as playing video games.

Procrastination is a problem that many of us face. Almost everyone has their particular issues that cause people to delay. Unfortunately, 20% of the population identifies themselves as chronic procrastinators. These are only the individuals that identify themselves as this as well. Remember, the first part of controlling procrastination is realizing that there is a problem in the first place. Many of these individuals don't ever get to the realization part, because no one is there to tell them or they just don't see a need to change. There are so many great goals that people have, and procrastination keeps them from achieving those goals.

WHY DO PEOPLE PROCRASTINATE?

Procrastinators can be broken down into different types and different combinations of these types. People even go through stages with different forms of procrastination depending on what is happening.

Their actions follow particular plans and for most procrastinators there is something they need.

HOW DO PEOPLE PROCRASTINATE?

The chronic delay is not typically a problem of time management or planning. The problem is finding distractions that can delay work but do not require a lot of commitment. Examples would be checking email or organizing things that are not important. The problem is actually chronic avoidance. You are avoiding taking productive action.

WHAT ARE THE CONSEQUENCES?

The obvious is that things that need to get completed either do not get done or they are done in a hurry. Sometimes when things are done at the last minute, you do not take the time to make your best effort, which is reflected in your work. This can, in the end, cost you jobs, grades, relationships and more.

CAN FRIENDS HELP ME STOP PROCRASTINATING?

Often times procrastination includes creating plenty of excuses that friends and family may allow which continues the cycle. You can ask those you care about to be firm when you break your schedules and mini goals. This would help you, but even then they may be soft when you do not complete what you need.

WHAT CAN I DO TO STOP PROCRASTINATING?

The easiest way to not procrastinate is to learn about your procrastination style and what it is you need. The second is to put your darn phone down. Lock it in another room and forget about it. Also, you can sit alone, in a quiet space and ask yourself why you procrastinate. Then listen for an answer. Ask yourself what is the advantage, and again wait and listen for an answer. Ask what you need to do to stop procrastinating and listen. Your body knows the answers and those answers may surprise you. Once you know the problems it will be easier to stop your procrastination and start doing.

Do you procrastinate because of...?

1. Fear of failure or success
2. Fear of rejection
3. Lack of knowledge on how to proceed
4. You don't like the task
5. Lack of time

Once you understand why you are procrastinating you can design a plan of action. If you are afraid of failure or rejection, just grab the bull by the horns and complete the task to the best of your ability. Design a step-by-step system on how to complete the task. If you do not have the required knowledge, seek out the guidance of a friend or a coach. Together you can work on completing the task. If you do not like to perform the task or do not have the time to complete it, consider hiring someone or asking for help to complete the task. If you REALLY don't have the time, then consider whether or not your other tasks are just as, if not more important.

Once the task is completed or delegated, you will feel a sense of accomplishment. You will be growing personally and a professional. So, stop procrastinating. Stop talking and start doing. Take Action.

WHY DO PEOPLE CHOOSE TO PROCRASTINATE?

Now, we all procrastinate from time to time. It's only when procrastination stops or hinders us from leading a full and vibrant life that it becomes a problem.

Some of us procrastinate at work with admin tasks, while some of us at home with household chores. Did you know that a form of procrastination is not paying your bills on time? (Assuming you have the means to do so). People may miss job or promotion opportunities; they may not appeal against parking fines on time or they may leave their Christmas or birthday gift shopping until the last minute. These are all real forms of procrastination and the consequences are always worse.

Procrastinators may tell themselves "I'll do this tomorrow" or "I work best under pressure." But the truth is procrastinators may put off doing things indefinitely - how many times have you heard someone say "I'll go on a diet tomorrow."? There are many ways to disrupt our lives but one of the worst ways, in my opinion, is procrastination. After all, who wants a life full of regrets through not taking action on time?

It is generally thought that we learn to procrastinate rather than we are born with it. Procrastination can be learned from one's parents, siblings or other figures of authority as we are growing up.

It is sometimes a response to an authoritarian

parenting style. Having controlling parents may keep children from developing the ability to take immediate action without seeking some extra guidance from an authority figure in their lives. As we then become adults we may still be seeking that extra guidance before we act, but at this point, the authority figures may not be present, which in turn leads us to put off or defer taking action.

In some cases, procrastination may be a form of rebellion or even a way of simply being noticed. Procrastinators may turn to friends rather than family for support, but unfortunately, our friends may actually justify the problem by accepting our excuses.

There are several effects of procrastination: Health for instance.. Studies have shown that procrastination may lead to a compromised immune system with more colds and flu, as well as more gastrointestinal problems and insomnia.

Procrastination may also shift the burden of responsibility away from us and onto others, and in doing so leads to resentfulness and may destroy teamwork and our relationships.

THERE ARE A NUMBER OF DIFFERENT TYPES OF PROCRASTINATORS:

1. Those seeking a high – these individuals leave things to the last minute and get a buzz from frantic last minute activities - especially when they have no options
2. Those with a fear of failure - The may even fear success, but either way this fear holds them back from the action. They may also be self-conscious and worry about what others may think of them.
3. Those who simply want to avoid making decisions. In this way, they take no responsibility for the outcome.

Now, if you're like me, and want to get rid of procrastination from your life completely, there are a number of techniques available, which we will cover later.

With concentrated effort, it is possible for procrastinators to beat their procrastination on their own. It will take a lot of mental energy and can be very draining. However, just because it's difficult, doesn't mean it's not worth it. Don't procrastinate on getting rid of your procrastination habits!

CHAPTER THREE

WAYS TO STOP PROCRASTINATING NOW

1. Procrastination emancipation: Once you've fully understood that one of the biggest reasons you have been procrastinating is that you're focusing only on finishing (and that's too daunting) you'll begin to instead concentrate on starting, which is a much more approachable and manageable way to get the thing done. All you need to do is keep starting, and finishing will take care of itself.

2. Procrastination transformation: Nothing helps you achieve more easily than knowing all the steps you need to take, having a plan to take them, scheduling that plan into your calendar, creating incentives to make following through more attractive (and consequences to make it less attractive!), and putting some accountability supports into place. This, combined with a simple procrastination meditation, will get you back on track quickly and easily.

3. Procrastination consultation: Talk with friends about how they overcame procrastination. Buddy up with them on their own projects, holding each other accountable to get things done. Hire a procrastination coach, someone

who has worked with hundreds of people and not only knows about procrastination generation but has helped many veteran procrastinators with procrastination renunciation.

4. Procrastination exploration: What is your procrastination costing you? Do you have a procrastination reputation? Do you continually have to make procrastination explanations or reparations to others? Are you in procrastination isolation so nobody will know what you're not doing? Is your credit history in procrastination degradation because of paying bills late? Are you in procrastination desperation because you might lose your job or significant relationships? Sometimes understanding how badly you're paying and in exactly what ways can provoke you to seek assistance.

5. Procrastination perspiration: You may think that the only way to stop procrastinating is to use willpower and discipline. While that certainly can work, it can cost you a lot of energy and struggle.

6. By allowing yourself to begin recognizing what is specifically in the way of following through and creating simple new patterns, progress can be pretty painless and immediate.

7. Procrastination inclination: At the moment you are about to procrastinate, stop for just a moment to acknowledge the pattern, even if you continue on to put off whatever you were going to do. Awareness and

acceptance that these are your current patterns is a necessary step in procrastination extermination.

8. Procrastination alienation: Recognize that you're not alone, and are, in fact, in excellent company. Most people procrastinate about something, sometimes about many things. In a recent survey on procrastination, almost 1/3 of respondents who identified themselves as procrastinators had a post-graduation or higher education.

9. Procrastination temptation: If you hang out with people who coax you to procrastinate, it's time to start surrounding yourself with better examples. If you know that certain situations are too enticing and will lure you from following through, create a workaround plan that will help you prevent yourself from "taking the bait".

10. Procrastination exaggeration: Are you really procrastinating, or are you simply focusing on other priorities? It's possible that those things you're not doing shouldn't get done until sometime later, perhaps not at all. Focus on only the most significant areas first, and the rest will come.

11. Procrastination condemnation: Lose the labels! All those things you call yourself, such as lazy, scattered, disorganized, not good enough, incompetent, or stupid, for example, aren't helping you get things done, are they? You've learned to believe them, and you think they've become something of a self-fulfilling prophecy. If you look around yourself, though, you'll see evidence that

you can accomplish quite a number of things without delay.

HOW TO BEAT PROCRASTINATION USING THIS 3-STEP PROCESS

You can literally say, "Goodbye Procrastination". Now, that might sound too simple, but it really is that simple; simple but very effective! What I'm suggesting is that you learn to "Externalize It!"

TRY THIS 3-STEP PROCESS TO EXTERNALIZE, ELIMINATE, & DETERMINE

1.   EXTERNALIZE PROCRASTINATION

Externalizing, in the therapeutic sense, means to make a mental projection, in image form, outside of oneself, and it is a method for counseling that is used in Narrative Therapy. It is a very useful therapeutic 'tool' for reducing self-blame and allows clients to create space for re-framing and restructuring self-identity. Therapists and counselors alike may tailor their use of externalization for a much broader spectrum.

We don't often call it by name directly, more often we indirectly speak of or think about it (i.e., "I should do this, but..." or "I can't seem to get to that project, maybe later...") only to wonder "why" we can't follow through and accomplish our goals. We know we "hate it" and "want it gone," but it seems that we surely haven't become great experts when it comes to saying goodbye to it for good.

So, if you view Procrastination as an entity outside yourself...someone else or something else...it can greatly help you to get past the feelings of "I am a 'bad' procrastinator" or something of the like. When you externalize, you essentially relieve yourself of the burden because the "Procrastinator" or "Procrastination" is outside yourself...It is NOT YOU! So, that means that the next time you find yourself struggling with your time management and feel procrastination is directing your actions, you can stop blaming yourself and sabotaging your belief in yourself to change your behaviors. You are not "The Procrastinator" and "The Procrastinator" is not your identity! Period.

Perhaps look at it like this: "I am learning now that procrastination can no longer be in my life and my choices will not be made to benefit procrastination anymore!

I am me and it has to leave now!" Make a mental picture of procrastination (create a specific vision in your mind) and watch procrastination literally walk through a doorway and out of your life."

Externalizing "Procrastination" allows you to release it and the inner grip that it once had on you. Procrastination does not have to be your resident arch nemesis any longer. If you try viewing it as separate from yourself, can begin to have the upper hand, free of the frustration it brought with it. However, the work doesn't stop here...

2.   ELIMINATE RESISTANCE

Once you decide to release it, you need to begin to eliminate its companion, which is resistance. Much of your procrastinating behavior is grounded in 'mental resistance,' so it makes sense to find a way to create space for a new mindset. You can even repeat Step 1 now and externalize "Resistance" ("It" now has a name, too). Let it go out the same doorway as procrastination!

The bottom line is: You've been battling two fierce

opponents and it seems that the more any of us 'resist' the more we procrastinate, and the stronger "Resistance and Procrastination" become, taking over our very existence. So, how do you fight off resistance?

Start using affirmations to help you eliminate resistance. Use your words and create an action to accomplish this. For instance, you could say, "I am no longer allowing resistance and procrastination to rent space in my head and use up my mental energy," or, "I am watching resistance and procrastination leave me now". Or, you might take a slightly different approach and say, "I am free to choose procrastination and resistance as friends (or perhaps teachers) so that I can learn more about why they held me back and why I fought with them and myself to get things done!"

Also, to eliminate resistance, you need to become aware of its presence. It's sneaky if you're not paying attention. Resistance will make your body feel terrible. Any response you have to a negative feeling is your body's attempt to send you the "red flag" that it is in motion. What you may or may not realize is that you get to control your "resistance gauge" and if you don't want it, you can let your thoughts overcome it.

Again, use your words and say, "I am feeling anxious right now, and that tells me that resistance is trying to come back into my life. There isn't room for you, Resistance. I am at peace here without you." The more you say it, and believe it, and feel it, the more you can lower that heartbeat and your anxiety will start to dissipate.

Taken a step further, resistance is a by-product of fear. Fear is not as easy to externalize, so we need to expand the search for answers by looking at the underlying fear that initiated your resistance that resulted in allowing procrastination and resistance to rent space in your mind.

3. DETERMINE YOUR FEAR

Begin to ask yourself what you felt the last time resistance led to procrastinating behavior. Did you feel anxious, afraid, confused, frustrated, or angry? Maybe all of the above? Think about this and really try to dig deep into the process of your procrastinating behavior. Step three is an important piece of this puzzle, so start by considering these three questions:

1. Am I fearful of rejection by others if I follow through with this goal or task?

2. Am I fearful of not knowing all the answers going in, so it's better to lack the initiative than it is to attempt and fail?

3. Am I fearful of letting go of Procrastination because it has protected me and if I freely give up something that has become valuable to me, won't I feel lost without it?

This should jump-start personal self reflection if you really want to look to the source of your fear. Remember: "Your fear is what led to your resistance that enabled procrastination." It's never an easy process to look inside and become acutely aware of negative emotions and behaviors. But, if you start this process by letting go of your identity as "The Procrastinator" or "A Procrastinator," you've made the first giant step in learning to "Externalize, Eliminate and Determine" your way to success.

CHAPTER FOUR

IS IT LAZINESS?

I for one am guilty of procrastination and used to think of myself as lazy. However, one evening as I lay on the sofa and I recounted my very busy day in my head - I needed that justification for having not started my very important writing assignment. I realized that in essence, I was not lazy at all.

In my search for answers, the one thing that I did discover is that I am not alone. I have been closely observing my friends and family and discovered that most people procrastinate to some degree or other. The degree at which people procrastinate varies from the most chronic procrastinator who never seems to achieve anything - for a variety of 'good' reasons real or unreal, to the mild procrastinator who can at least admit and notice when procrastination is taking place and do something about it.

WHY DO WE PUT OFF IMPORTANT TASKS THROUGH PROCRASTINATION?

I found this to be most perplexing. My task was important to me, I was eager and keen - yet I found I was never in the right mood; the place was too messy, or I had things to do. The phone is ringing and I had better answer it or... or what? Why was I making everything else so much more important than that what I wanted to do?

The dictionary definition of procrastination is the act of postponing, delaying or putting off, especially out of habitual carelessness or laziness.

So, basically procrastination refers to the act of replacing high-priority actions with tasks of low-priority, and so putting off important tasks to a later time. This is exactly what I was doing; I wasn't being lazy after all! Or was I?

A procrastinator needs to address 'why the task is being put off'. The identifying reason alone will be the motivating force to take action and complete the task at hand. In essence, procrastination is a thief of time.

Time management experts may say write a 'to do list' and tick them off as you go. However, if you are like me, I can tick off things and still avoid the one thing that was really important to do because obviously, it can go on tomorrow's list. Yet when tomorrow comes another day dawns, and other things still always seem to take priority.

Procrastinators are not born this way. They are made over the course of time. The procrastination habit can be learned within the family and in the school of life. But I believe not directly, it is a learned action more by submitting to a pressure or a fear of failure.

Learned behaviors can be unlearned, so procrastinators can change - one small step at a time.

Why do we attach 'no importance' to very important tasks?

Believe it or not, procrastinators actually tell lies to themselves. They do not see themselves in their true light; they say things like "I'll feel more like doing this tomorrow." Or "I'll work best after a good night's sleep." But in reality, they do not get the urge the next day or work best after rest. Plus, they justify themselves by saying "this isn't really that important". Procrastinators can actually squander their resources. When you put something off once, it makes it that much easier to do it again.

There are many ways to self-sabotage your success in life and procrastination is one choice of the path that people take without even realizing they are doing it. Procrastinating behavior can be actions taken to avoid the fear of failure or even fear of success. Some procrastinators are very concerned with what others think of them; they would rather have others think they lack effort, rather than ability. By not making decisions, procrastinators absolve themselves of the responsibility for the outcome of events. This was exactly what my personal problem was, and it wasn't easy to overcome.

There can be big costs to procrastination. Health is one, as well as a productive life. Procrastination can lead to guilt, stress, and insomnia, which can, in turn, lead to severe loss of personal productivity as well strain in personal relationships. It has a tendency to shift the burden of responsibilities onto others, who may then become resentful. Therefore, it is very important to try to modify or reduce this behavior as much as possible and as soon as possible.

You can change this prevailing and self-sabotaging behavior with a few simple steps.

Traditionally, procrastination has been associated with the following tendencies:

- Perfectionism, which is a tendency to negatively evaluate outcomes and one's own performance.
- An intense fear and avoidance of evaluation of one's abilities by others.
- Heightened social self-consciousness and anxiety,
- Recurrent low mood.

Exploring why you procrastinate is the first step towards a transformation. There can be many reasons for example; fear, dislike, pressure, boredom, and avoidance of responsibility. This habit has been developed over a long period of time, so the change will take time too. You can change your behavior; just don't expect to change it overnight.

You can experiment with different strategies as the same strategy does not work for everyone.

Try some of these useful tips:

- Break down large tasks or projects into smaller chunks.

- Reward yourself for small successes - you deserve it
- Do not punish yourself when you do procrastinate. You will eventually develop new habits with new feelings of self-confidence and achievement. Instead, ask yourself if the consequence of procrastinating was really worth it.
- If you are finding this to be difficult, then you know it's worth doing. Enlist the help of an 'Anti-Procrastinator Coach' who is typically a close good friend you have confided in who will alert you when they find you procrastinating.
- Start on your important task of the day FIRST and follow on later with all those other less important tasks of the day.

In brief, most procrastinators are not lazy but have the ability to do all sorts of other tasks in order to put off the most 'important task' of the day. This is accomplished for a variety of reasons, most of which are not reasons but excuses. Being a self-confessed procrastinator myself, I know it is not always intentional, and in some cases subconscious, but once it is recognized you now have the ability to stop in your tracks and set it straight.

In my opinion, the way to 'solve' the problem of procrastination is to enjoy the pull of achievement by not putting off the 'important task' but by putting off the 'less important tasks' that can be left undone.

These feelings of achievement are the feelings that will help you drive the changes to your behavior.

So, stop procrastinating and take action and start doing. As Alexander Graham Bell once said, "The only difference between success and failure is the ability to take action."

CHAPTER FIVE

HOW TO END PROCRASTINATION

1.   TIME MANAGEMENT

If you're struggling with procrastination, you know that you want to end the struggle and overcome it. I know you think you're not good at time management. Procrastination is wrecking your life, whether you know it or not. If not wrecking, then hindering your ability to be the best and most efficient version of yourself.

These strategies, followed in order and really put to use, will help you overcome your procrastination.

What you'll learn is that it's not really all about time management. Procrastination is a mental block, a paralysis that takes hold of us and makes us think we're lazy and worthless when in reality we're none of those things.

That's what makes these strategies so powerful. They get to the root of the procrastination and eliminates it so you can go forward as a person with a purpose.

1.   Identify what's going on: It may be procrastination. You may be putting things off without a good reason. On the other hand, you may have very good reasons for changing the time and order when you do things. You may be ill, or you may be changing priorities. You may be waiting on someone else. Or, you may have just decided something doesn't need doing. None of that is procrastination. But if you are procrastinating, you can do something about it.

2.   Relax: Although what you're experiencing is stressful, it is important that you find a way to relax and stop letting the stress build up. Stress only leads to more procrastination. Take some time to just not think about time management, procrastination or any of the difficulties you're facing because of this burden.

3.   Do triage: Be very honest with yourself about what you have outstanding, what you can complete and what you can't complete. This will not be easy but it is very, very necessary. If you're like me and 99% of the people I work with, there are things you can't complete on your current list. Being honest about this is the most important step in time management procrastination elimination. Wow, say that five times fast...

4.   Release: Let go of the projects you cannot complete. This may be unpleasant, but the hard part won't take long

and you'll be free to go on to the next step, which is much more pleasant and much easier.

5. Reaffirm: Now you need to recommit to the projects and tasks you can and will complete. At this point, you're just making a commitment, but soon you'll figure out how to get all of it done.

6. Strategize: Create a time management procrastination avoidance plan that will help you get everything done without procrastinating.

7. Implement: Now put your plan into action and go forward as a person who does not procrastinate.

These strategies will help you become a person who avoids procrastination before it even begins.

2. HYPNOSIS

Another way to treat and end procrastination once and for all is to train your mind to work with the subconscious where permanent changes are activated and self-sabotaging thoughts and behaviors are eliminated for good. Procrastination Hypnosis is a unique, yet innovative approach to ending procrastination that does just that.

How can Procrastination Hypnosis solve your procrastination problem? To fully appreciate this, indulge in some positive procrastination to understand why you procrastinate and are so jolly lazy, lying around doing diddly squat, wasting time and ignoring the chores. This is okay for a bit, but the real danger is when it becomes a way of life.

Has it got to stage with you yet? Are you chronically lazy, putting things off, don't pay the bills on time or even worse, stay in a job you HATE? Procrastinators waste time doing nothing even though they are well aware that things need doing. But for some reason, they just don't do it. Then the snowballing effect wacks you in the back of your head and tiny tasks become massive. What a travesty this can become if you don't make the effort to get over yourself and end procrastination. You can miss out on so much of life. Is that what you want?

Have you ever been told you're lazy, a waste of space, ineffective or unreliable? Hmm, perhaps not to your face? Failure to deal with procrastination stands between you and a productive, fuller life and only launches you further along the downward, spiraling slide to an empty, unfulfilling life where frustration and powerlessness is your constant companion.

HOW TO PROCRASTINATION HYPNOSIS CAN END

PROCRASTINATION

This is an effective way is to make your mind aware of and deal with it on a subconscious level by reprogramming your thought patterns and eliminating sabotaging behaviors. It's a proven treatment for procrastination that eliminates it for good.

The reason this works so effectively is that chronic procrastination or laziness is a psychological issue that is often deeply ingrained over many years. Procrastination Hypnosis makes changes at the subconscious level, eliminates deeply ingrained patterns and ends procrastination for good. Additionally, it's surprisingly simple.

This change at the subconscious level is the solution to reprogramming your mind and setting it back on course. As Neil Armstrong's small step on the moon was a huge step for mankind, this small step could be a huge leap for your new improved life from here on out.

THE EFFECTS OF HYPNOSIS

There is truly no need to continue on the

procrastination cycle of a wait, wait, wait, stress out, and wait some more. You can overcome procrastination. How? Through the power of hypnosis.

Hypnosis is not some hocus pocus form of psychotherapy - it is simply a naturally occurring state of mind that bypasses the conscious part of the mind. When the conscious is bypassed, we don't pass judgment on what is being suggested.

Believe it or not, we are in a hypnotic state quite often. For instance, here are some times when you have "turned off" the judgment portion of your mind:

When you see a commercial on TV that influences you to buy a product.

When an expert tells you something and you don't question the validity of that statement.

Children do it when they are pretending.

By going around the judgment portion of the mind, suggestions can be put into your subconscious and lead you towards a particular goal - just the way advertisers propel you towards their product.

Hypnosis can help you overcome procrastination forever. How? By detouring around your conscious mind!

Procrastination is nothing more than a bad habit. Your conscious mind doesn't like change and will "talk" you right out of changing. However, if you can get those suggestions into your subconscious mind without the judgmental filter, you can change from being a procrastinator to being an achiever.

Hypnosis and meditation is stronger than willpower because it puts the suggestions straight into your subconscious, the way advertisers do. By the time the suggestions reach your conscious mind, they will have already been accepted by your subconscious - so no more defeating self-talk to contend with!

Best of all, your changed status from procrastinator to achiever means that you will achieve your goals and still have time left over. Instead of using up all your spare time with worry, guilt, and frustration, you can use your spare time for enjoyment and relaxation!

THE WAY I SEE IT, YOU'VE GOT TWO OPTIONS;

a. Let life control you by doing nothing. Continue along the path to an empty, unfulfilled life full of frustration and feelings of powerlessness because you won't make the decision to take the necessary action to end your procrastination problem.

b. Take control of your life. Get a grip on yourself, beat procrastination and create a life you actually want instead of allowing life to control you by default.

Procrastination is a killer - a killer of dreams, ambitions, and achievement.

My question to you, is what are you going to do now?

CHAPTER SIX

FIVE EMPOWERING PROCRASTINATION TIPS

One of the most destructive effects of procrastination is the fact that it makes you feel out of control. Procrastination is like an invisible force that keeps you from doing the very things you know you must do. With the increasing demands on our time and attention, there seems to be an increase in procrastination as a chronic problem, especially amongst those people that want to succeed the most. Procrastination usually sets in when you feel overwhelmed by all the 'have to's' in life, and instead of making steady progress you take on too much without ever getting any of it done.

Feeling out of control takes away all your power to shape and direct your own life. It's true that there are many things over which you have no control, but you always have full control over what you ultimately become - and what really happens to you is a mental process independent of the circumstances and events of the outside world. Being empowered means that you realize that you already have the power and this realization also gives you the ability to take action. Here are five empowering procrastination tips that can help you to reach this realization and become empowered to effectively deal with procrastination and inaction.

1. IT'S ALL INTERNAL

Procrastination is an internal process and although it might feel like it's happening to you, you are in fact responsible for it. This procrastination tip can help to put you back in control almost immediately. Procrastination is not an external force, but an internal response and evaluation. The simple realization that it's 'you' that's doing it to 'you', gives you the power to do something about it.

2. IT'S ALL YOU

When procrastination drags you down, it's all too easy to think that 'it just is what it is' and that you can't do anything about it. Although it feels like you have no control, you actually do. In fact, this is why you feel out of control - because you believe that you can't do anything about it. There are two very important beliefs you need to develop to help you break free from procrastination.

The first is that you CAN overcome procrastination and the second is that YOU can overcome procrastination. No one else can do it for you and because you created it; you can un-create it.

3. IT'S ALL IN YOUR HEAD

The reason why most people remain stuck in patterns of procrastination is that of fear. At the most fundamental level, all forms of procrastination come down to fear, and the anxiety that stems from that fear. What you don't face ultimately controls you. To overcome the fear and the procrastination that comes with it, you need to confront and do the very things you don't want to do. The instant you do, you take charge and it no longer has any control over you. The ironic thing is that fear only exists in your imagination - it's always something that hasn't happened yet. Procrastination is not real - it's only the way you evaluate fear in your mind.

4. IT'S ALL ABOUT CONDITIONING

Success at anything in life relies on consistency. The

best of the best at anything are those who can repeat their greatness consistently. The way you become consistent is through conditioning. Your nervous system operates through conditioning. When you do something over and over again it becomes 'normal' and when it's normal you don't have to think about it - it becomes automatic. The challenge is that this principle works both ways. Whether your conditioned responses support you or whether it pulls you down, your nervous system does not make that distinction. If procrastination is your conditioned response you will always feel out of control, simply because that's what you've 'learned' to do automatically. You simply need to 'recondition' yourself to a new response; to teach yourself to respond in a different way...

5.   IT'S ALL ABOUT AWARENESS

Procrastination does serve a purpose - and a very important one at that, but only if you are aware of the benefits. We only procrastinate about those things that have value to us. At some level, either directly or indirectly, you believe that taking action will benefit you. If it didn't it wouldn't bother you, right? Be grateful for procrastination and use it as a guide to 'know' what you need to act upon.

Being aware of this fact, and developing awareness of what you do and fail to do can empower you to be in charge of yourself on a much higher level.

When you are empowered you are in charge, and even if things seem to go wrong on the surface, underneath you know that you have the power to deal with it effectively on your own terms. Procrastination is disempowering and it takes away your ability to take immediate action and deal with any situation. Always remember that you are ultimately in charge of you. Tomorrow will be today, tomorrow. Don't delay. Act!

CHAPTER SEVEN

MANY NEGATIVE EFFECTS OF PROCRASTINATION

The Negative Effects of Procrastination take place in all of your major life areas:

Relationships with Your Spouse or Significant Other

Relationships with Your Children

Work or Business

Health

Finances

How are each of these areas affected by your lack of action?

Let's take a look at 5 areas of your life and how procrastinating affects it.

A. ADVERSE EFFECTS OF RELATIONSHIPS WITH YOUR SPOUSE OR SIGNIFICANT OTHER

You love your partner. You truly do, but do they know it?

Do you keep thinking that you should send them flowers, take them to dinner or do something nice just because?

Do you promise that you will do stuff together and you just never get around to it?

Do you promise that you will complete your house to-do list but you keep putting it off?

If you answered yes to any of these questions, I want you to think. What are you doing to your relationship with your significant other?

Maybe they are irritated with you. Then, you become irritated with them.

What could be the big negative effect of procrastination? You break up. Now, if you're not married, you might think that's no big deal. There are other fish in the sea and so on and so forth. Really?

What happens when you do the same thing to your next partner? Now, if you are married, think about the expense and stress of an escalated event.

B. NEGATIVE SIDE EFFECTS OF PROCRASTINATION IN RELATIONSHIPS WITH YOUR CHILDREN

If you don't have kids, skip this one and go to the next section. If you do have kids, what kind of example are you setting for them? They see you putting stuff off so why wouldn't they put their chores and school work off?

Now, what happens if you have procrastinated in setting up your will and you pass away?

If you have loads of debt because you put off getting your finances in order, what kind of legacy are you leaving them behind? People don't think about these things because they are unpleasant. However, it's beneficial to do so.

C. DEBILITATING EFFECTS OF YOUR BUSINESS

You know there are a few things you must do in your business in order for it to grow or even get started.

For me, they are meeting people, putting out content, and communicating with my list. There are other things too, but nothing will happen if I don't do those three basic things.

Now, imagine you decided you'll just do that basic task tomorrow. When you finally do get around to it, how many days did you waste? Is it a month later?

How the heck are you going to build a business if you can't even hold yourself to do the bare minimum?

Don't let this be you.

D. HOW DOES PROCRASTINATION AFFECT YOUR HEALTH?

What if you have skipped having your regular checkups? Then, one day, God forbid, you find something. The doctor tells you that either it's too late or that you need to schedule something quickly.

Don't continue to put off eating healthy or exercising until tomorrow. What if tomorrow doesn't come? It's hard to think about but these are real scenarios. No one ever thinks it will happen to them until it does.

E.   NEGATIVE EFFECTS OF PROCRASTINATION ON YOUR FINANCES

Imagine you keep saying that you will pay your bills tomorrow. Now, mind you, you do have the money, but you just keep procrastinating on paying them.

Some of those late payment fees can be upwards of 35 bucks! How much a month are you paying because of your procrastination?

So what do you do now?

I suggest you write down five things that you have been procrastinating on in each area of your life.

Then, set some time aside and do them.

Make a game out of it. How?

Put on a song and see how far or how much you can do in one of your areas affected by procrastinating.

Get a buddy. Tell someone what you are going to do and have them hold you accountable.

Those are just a few suggestions of how to get rid of

the negative effects of procrastination. Brainstorm and find some more. Procrastination can really destroy your life if you let it.

STOP PROCRASTINATION AND SUCCEED

No matter who you are, it happens to the best of us. We can all make excuses for not doing what we know we should do or want to do. Procrastination can affect us all. New Year's resolutions are all well and good if you achieve them. Many people find that they are no further ahead this year with their aims and ambitions than they were last year.

If you have felt that nagging sense that things are the same and the positive changes you crave don't happen, you may be suffering from the habit of procrastination.

A.   PROCRASTINATION IN YOUR OCCUPATION

Are you someone who is always late to work or appointments because your motivation is missing. Do you lose hours at work doing non-essential jobs and avoid getting going with the tasks you know you should be doing? A vicious cycle can start for you. The more you delay starting that new project or priority task, the more pressure you will feel and the more likely you are to avoid it and procrastinate. Some people even change employers and jobs to avoid having to start or complete a project that they have prevaricated over.

You may be bored in your current job but the security of it keeps you from leaving and you feel trapped. The fear of what a new job might involve may stop you from applying for new jobs and getting a role that could re-motivate you. All the time you delay, your self-confidence is being eroded and your ability to procrastinate grows.

B. PERSONAL LIFE PROCRASTINATION

Have you stayed in your relationship because it provides familiarity and a sense of safety? Has your relationship lost its spark and you and your partner have settled into a safe and yet boring rut? This can happen in any relationship and it doesn't mean that you have to end it. The best relationship for you may be the one that you are currently in. Unless you are present in the relationship and appreciate it, you may feel unhappy, lost or just trapped. Procrastination can become of feature of personal relationships too.

C.   DOMESTIC PROCRASTINATION

Are the numbers of domestic jobs at home building up? Does your home need some repair or maintenance such as a cupboard that needs fixing or a leaky pipe that needs to be repaired? Sometimes even calling in a contractor to fix a domestic problem can lead to procrastination. Instead of it being a simple job, not fixing it in time makes for a more expensive repair in the future. You may have outstanding bills that you have not settled or other legal or challenging matters that need your attention but you have yet to tackle them.

Your home should be a place where you can unwind and relax, yet you may find that your home is no longer that safe and secure haven. The unstated or unfinished jobs around your home just add to a sense of drift as the years go by and nothing changes.

Procrastination can have a negative affect on many areas of our lives. Yet, you don't have to keep putting up with a life of malaise. If you envy others' success, it means you recognize things can be different and you can change too. Yet, procrastination is often just a state of mind that anyone can fall victim to and recover from.

Maybe you have tried and (apparently) failed to change before. Maybe you have convinced yourself that whatever you do, nothing will improve for you. There is a common negative saying that you may be familiar with: "I should accept my lot". If you have used it yourself then stop it now. It doesn't serve you in any way other than to keep you trapped as you are. Don't use it as a justification for misfortunes.

STOP YOUR PROCRASTINATION

Understanding procrastination can also provide the clues to escaping from it too. Initially, take things one step at a time. Don't put pressure on yourself by aiming for too many goals. This approach can overwhelm you. Keep it simple to start with and aim for tasks, goals, and achievements that are easy for you. Small and easy goals are more likely to be achieved. In reaching your sense of success, no matter how small, you are more likely to then be able to achieve bigger and longer term goals.

Start today by viewing yourself differently and quit using any negative self-labels. If you view yourself succeeding and doing those tasks and jobs, you are much more likely to succeed (research has shown this). If you label yourself with names such as useless, lazy, or other unhelpful adjectives, it will undermine your ability to motivate yourself and make those all important changes.

If you change how you imagine yourself to be, and drop the negative labels, you will find it easier to make progress.

Procrastination is not something you neccesarily inherited, but something that may have been influenced by others. Procrastination is a habit but it doesn't have to be a way of life.

As human beings, we are very adaptable and change habits all the time. Just a little bit of work can support your decision to stop procrastinating. Rather than feeling like a victim of it, take control of your life.

CHAPTER EIGHT

PROCRASTINATION AS A CAREER KILLER

Are you a procrastinator? Do you know a procrastinator? If you're not sure, here are some ways you can tell if you or someone you know is a procrastinator:

There are many reasons that a person may procrastinate, such as:

1. Fear: Anxiety plays a large factor in procrastination. When someone feels anxious about a task it's likely because they think they'll fail, or because they're not quite sure how to approach the task to even begin. The feeling of being overwhelmed comes into play here as well. If the individual feels the task is too large to handle, or they don't have enough time to complete it, they may become overwhelmed with the process, creating a sense of fear.

2. Not knowing where to start: This is quite common among procrastinators. If they don't even know where to start on a project, then they will put the project off as long as possible because they just can't wrap their head around where to begin.

3. Too difficult: The difficulty of the task may vary, but generally the more difficult the task the more likely it'll be put off by a procrastinator. A procrastinator would prefer to complete simpler and more pleasurable activities first to give them the instant satisfaction of a job well done.

So, how can procrastination be a career killer? Here are a few examples:

Consistently completing tasks or projects after the due date can create an impression among supervisors and coworkers that the individual isn't reliable or dependable.

A procrastinator will be overlooked for major projects that could give them an advantage in the workplace because they won't be seen as trustworthy.

Rushing to complete projects at the last minute can cause mistakes, an unfinished or unpolished professional look, and won't be taken lightly by a boss or team member.

Work ethics will be called out if the projects aren't created at a certain level of expectations.

A procrastinator will be viewed as someone who just makes excuses and doesn't create quality work consistently.

Even with just one or two of these examples, a supervisor may choose to use, promote, and applaud others and leave the procrastinator in the dust in regard to increased responsibilities, advancement, raises, and promotions.

HOW DO YOU (OR SOMEONE YOU KNOW) FIX IT?

a.   Begin working immediately: create a plan. Figure out the specific steps of what needs to happen to complete the task - and write them down as a plan of action. Creating an action plan will help reduce the fear of tackling the project and will help reduce the procrastination time.

b.   Enlist help: Follow-up with a supervisor, team member, or coworker on specific tasks you need help with that they can easily complete. Ask for completion or submission dates for their specific tasks so you know when to expect them. Having assistance will help hold the procrastinator responsible, and will share the weight of the project with others, reducing the anxiety and the fear of failure.

c. Break up the project: don't try tackling the entire project in one shot, especially if it's a large project. Create blocks of tasks that need to be done by a certain date and then list the next steps for the project. This will give the procrastinator a sense of accomplishment as each portion of the project is completed.

d. Be consistent: this is especially true while working with other team members. Show them that you are serious about completing the project on time and with quality. This will help hold everyone accountable, which will produce a much better outcome, and increase the ability to obtain promotions, raises, and recognition.

Procrastination is not something that will be 'cured' overnight. It will take work; it'll be quite frustrating at times, and some things may still slip through the cracks at times. But, as long as you (or the person you know) work at changing the way tasks and projects are handled and are more forward thinking, it'll get easier and easier as you move forward. Just take it one day at a time.

CONCLUSION

Chances are you procrastinate; nearly everyone does, nearly every day (it's one of the few things we don't put off till tomorrow!). Procrastination is a thief, and it's stealing from you on a daily basis. And what it's taking can never, ever be replaced. It steals your time, that most valuable commodity, that thing that's so precious that untold millions couldn't buy you a single minute's worth. Every time you put tasks off until tomorrow, you're letting that time slip away forever. It's time you'll never have again, and it carries opportunities with it, perhaps to never be seen again. Procrastination is the thief of time is an old saying, and a wise one. We would do well to take it to heart.

Many people waste time because they fear failure. For them, to try is to risk failing; therefore, it's easier to never try because then they never fail. You miss 100% of the shots you don't take. In other words, procrastination is saving them from failing. But not really. It's actually causing them to fail because they never try.

Once you figure out the emotional reason behind your procrastination, it's easier to fight. If you know why you waste time, then you either need to overcome that or find another way to satisfy that part of life. For instance, many people procrastinate because they're overworked and need a break. If this is the case, reevaluate your work schedule, you'll get way more done.

The best way to overcome procrastination is to use this emotional reason against yourself. To do this, you need to figure out why you procrastinate and then prove to yourself that procrastinating is causing you more pain or less pleasure depending on how you motivate yourself. While the way you procrastinate will tell you how you're motivated, it's far easier to just ask yourself how you wake up in the morning--are you motivated to get up and enjoy the day or because you really have to pee?

Another major reason for procrastination is a lack of desire. If you don't want to do the task, it's a lot harder to get it done. The real question to ask in that case is why do you put yourself through this? Do you fear the risk of trying something new? Why would you continue doing something you don't like? Because that's key; why do you procrastinate finding other, more enjoyable options for your time? Or, go the other way; work on enjoying what you do.

Procrastination is difficult to manage because we underestimate its accumulative effects and overestimate our ability to handle them. If we cannot eliminate procrastination from our lives entirely, the next best thing is to contain it. This means being aware of our procrastination and taking steps to deal with it. Through constant vigilance, we can manage procrastination effectively and maintain harmony in our lives.